Explainable AI Recipes

Implement Solutions to Model Explainability and Interpretability with Python

Pradeepta Mishra

Apress®

Explainable AI Recipes: Implement Solutions to Model Explainability and Interpretability with Python

Pradeepta Mishra
Bangalore, Karnataka, India

ISBN-13 (pbk): 978-1-4842-9028-6   ISBN-13 (electronic): 978-1-4842-9029-3
https://doi.org/10.1007/978-1-4842-9029-3

Managing Director, Apress Media LLC: Welmoed Spahr
Acquisitions Editor: Celestin Suresh John
Development Editor: James Markham
Coordinating Editor: Mark Powers
Copy Editor: Kim Wimpsett

Cover designed by eStudioCalamar

Cover image by Marek Piwinicki on Unsplash (www.unsplash.com)

Distributed to the book trade worldwide by Apress Media, LLC, 1 New York Plaza, New York, NY 10004, U.S.A. Phone 1-800-SPRINGER, fax (201) 348-4505, e-mail orders-ny@springer-sbm.com, or visit www.springeronline.com. Apress Media, LLC is a California LLC and the sole member (owner) is Springer Science + Business Media Finance Inc (SSBM Finance Inc). SSBM Finance Inc is a **Delaware** corporation.

For information on translations, please e-mail booktranslations@springernature.com; for reprint, paperback, or audio rights, please e-mail bookpermissions@springernature.com.

Apress titles may be purchased in bulk for academic, corporate, or promotional use. eBook versions and licenses are also available for most titles. For more information, reference our Print and eBook Bulk Sales web page at www.apress.com/bulk-sales.

Any source code or other supplementary material referenced by the author in this book is available to readers on GitHub (https://github.com/Apress). For more detailed information, please visit www.apress.com/source-code.

Printed on acid-free paper

I dedicate this book to my late father; my mother; my lovely wife, Prajna; and my daughters, Priyanshi (Aarya) and Adyanshi (Aadya). This work would not have been possible without their inspiration, support, and encouragement.

Table of Contents

About the Author

 **Pradeepta Mishra** is an AI/ML leader, experienced data scientist, and artificial intelligence architect. He currently heads NLP, ML, and AI initiatives for five products at FOSFOR by LTI, a leading-edge innovator in AI and machine learning based out of Bangalore, India. He has expertise in designing artificial intelligence systems for performing tasks such as understanding natural language and making recommendations based on natural language processing. He has filed 12 patents as an inventor and has authored and coauthored five books, including *R Data Mining Blueprints* (Packt Publishing, 2016), *R: Mining Spatial, Text, Web, and Social Media Data* (Packt Publishing, 2017), *PyTorch Recipes* (Apress, 2019), and *Practical Explainable AI Using Python* (Apress, 2023). There are two courses available on Udemy based on these books.

Pradeepta presented a keynote talk on the application of bidirectional LSTM for time-series forecasting at the 2018 Global Data Science Conference. He delivered the TEDx talk "Can Machines Think?" on the power of artificial intelligence in transforming industries and job roles across industries. He has also delivered more than 150 tech talks on data science, machine learning, and artificial intelligence at various meetups, technical institutions, universities, and community forums. He is on LinkedIn (www.linkedin.com/in/pradeepta/) and Twitter (@pradmishra1).

About the Technical Reviewer

 **Bharath Kumar Bolla** has more than ten years of experience and is currently working as a senior data science engineer consultant at Verizon, Bengaluru. He has a PG diploma in data science from Praxis Business School and an MS in life sciences from Mississippi State University. He previously worked as a data scientist at the University of Georgia, Emory University, and Eurofins LLC & Happiest Minds. At Happiest Minds, he worked on AI-based digital marketing products and NLP-based solutions in the education domain. Along with his day-to-day responsibilities, Bharath is a mentor and an active researcher. To date, he has published ten articles in journals and peer-reviewed conferences. He is particularly interested in unsupervised and semisupervised learning and efficient deep learning architectures in NLP and computer vision.

Acknowledgments

I would like to thank my wife, Prajna, for her continuous inspiration and support and for sacrificing her weekends to help me complete this book; and my daughters, Aarya and Aadya, for being patient throughout the writing process.

A big thank-you to Celestin Suresh John and Mark Powers for fast-tracking the whole process and guiding me in the right direction.

I would like to thank the authors of the Appliances Energy Prediction dataset (`http://archive.ics.uci.edu/ml`) for making it available: D. Dua and C. Graff. I use this dataset in the book to show how to develop a model and explain the predictions generated by a regression model for the purpose of model explainability using various explainable libraries.

Introduction

Artificial intelligence plays a crucial role determining the decisions businesses make. In these cases, when a machine makes a decision, humans usually want to understand whether the decision is authentic or whether it was generated in error. If business stakeholders are not convinced by the decision, they will not trust the machine learning system, and hence artificial intelligence adoption will gradually reduce within that organization. To make the decision process more transparent, developers must be able to document the explainability of AI decisions or ML model decisions. This book provides a series of solutions to problems that require explainability and interpretability. Adopting an AI model and developing a responsible AI system requires explainability as a component.

This book covers model interpretation for supervised learning linear models, including important features for regression and classification models, partial dependency analysis for regression and classification models, and influential data point analysis for both classification and regression models. Supervised learning models using nonlinear models is explored using state-of-the-art frameworks such as SHAP values/scores, including global explanation, and how to use LIME for local interpretation. This book will also give you an understanding of bagging, boosting-based ensemble models for supervised learning such as regression and classification, as well as explainability for time-series models using LIME and SHAP, natural language processing tasks such as text classification, and sentiment analysis using ELI5, ALIBI. The most complex models for classification and regression, such as neural network models and deep learning models, are explained using the CAPTUM framework, which shows feature attribution, neuron attribution, and activation attribution.

This book attempts to make AI models explainable to help developers increase the adoption of AI-based models within their organizations and bring more transparency to decision-making. After reading this book, you will be able to use Python libraries such as Alibi, SHAP, LIME, Skater, ELI5, and CAPTUM. *Explainable AI Recipes* provides a problem-solution approach to demonstrate each machine learning model, and shows how to use Python's XAI libraries to answer questions of explainability and build trust with AI models and machine learning models. All source code can be downloaded from `github.com/apress/explainable-ai-recipes`.

CHAPTER 1

Introducing Explainability and Setting Up Your Development Environment

Industries in which artificial intelligence has been applied include banking, financial services, insurance, healthcare, manufacturing, retail, and pharmaceutical. There are regulatory requirements in some of these industries where model explainability is required. Artificial intelligence involves classifying objects, recognizing objects to detect fraud, and so forth. Every learning system requires three things: input data, processing, and an output. If the performance of any learning system improves over time by learning from new examples or data, it is called a *machine learning system*. When the number of features for a machine learning task increases or the volume of data increases, it takes a lot of time to apply machine learning techniques. That's when deep learning techniques are used.

Figure 1-1 represents the relationships between artificial intelligence, machine learning, and deep learning.

© Pradeepta Mishra 2023
P. Mishra, *Explainable AI Recipes*, https://doi.org/10.1007/978-1-4842-9029-3_1

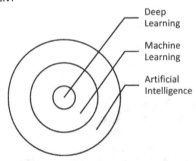

Figure 1-1. *Relationships among ML, DL, and AI*

After preprocessing and feature creation, you can observe hundreds
of thousands of features that need to be computed to produce output. If
we train a machine learning supervised model, it will take significant time
to produce the model object. To achieve scalability in this task, we need
deep learning algorithms, such as a recurrent neural network. This is how
artificial intelligence is connected to deep learning and machine learning.

In the classical predictive modeling scenario, a function is identified,
and the input data is usually fit to the function to produce the output,
where the function is usually predetermined. In a modern predictive
modeling scenario, the input data and output are both shown to a group of
functions, and the machine identifies the best function that approximates
well to the output given a particular set of input. There is a need to explain
the output of a machine learning and deep learning model in performing
regression- and classification-related tasks. These are the reasons why
explainability is required:

- *Trust*: To gain users' trust on the predicted output

- *Reliability*: To make the user rely on the
  predicted output

- *Regulatory*: To meet regulatory and compliance
  requirements

- *Adoption*: To increase AI adoption among the users

- *Fairness*: To remove any kind of discrimination in prediction

- *Accountability*: To establish ownership of the predictions

There are various ways that explainability can be achieved using statistical properties, probabilistic properties and associations, and causality among the features. Broadly, the explanations of the models can be classified into two categories, global explanations and local explanations. The objective of local explanation is to understand the inference generated for one sample at a time by comparing the nearest possible data point; global explanation provides an idea about the overall model behavior.

The goal of this chapter is to introduce how to install various explainability libraries and interpret the results generated by those explainability libraries.

Recipe 1-1. SHAP Installation
Problem

You want to install the SHAP (shapely additive explanations) library.

Solution

The solution to this problem is to use the simple pip or conda option.

How It Works

Let's take a look at the following script examples. The SHAP Python library is based on a game theoretic approach that attempts to explain local and as well as global explanations.

```
pip install shap
```

or

```
conda install -c conda-forge shap
```

```
Looking in indexes: https://pypi.org/simple, https://us-python.
pkg.dev/colab-wheels/public/simple/
Collecting shap
  Downloading shap-0.41.0-cp37-cp37m-manylinux_2_12_x86_64.
  manylinux2010_x86_64.whl (569 kB)
     |████████████████████████████████|
     |████████████████████| 569 kB 8.0 MB/s
Requirement already satisfied: tqdm>4.25.0 in /usr/local/lib/
python3.7/dist-packages (from shap) (4.64.1)
Requirement already satisfied: pandas in /usr/local/lib/
python3.7/dist-packages (from shap) (1.3.5)
Collecting slicer==0.0.7
  Downloading slicer-0.0.7-py3-none-any.whl (14 kB)
Requirement already satisfied: cloudpickle in /usr/local/lib/
python3.7/dist-packages (from shap) (1.5.0)
Requirement already satisfied: scipy in /usr/local/lib/
python3.7/dist-packages (from shap) (1.7.3)
Requirement already satisfied: scikit-learn in /usr/local/lib/
python3.7/dist-packages (from shap) (1.0.2)
Requirement already satisfied: numpy in /usr/local/lib/
python3.7/dist-packages (from shap) (1.21.6)
Requirement already satisfied: numba in /usr/local/lib/
python3.7/dist-packages (from shap) (0.56.2)
```

```
Requirement already satisfied: packaging>20.9 in /usr/local/
lib/python3.7/dist-packages (from shap) (21.3)
Requirement already satisfied: pyparsing!=3.0.5,>=2.0.2 in /
usr/local/lib/python3.7/dist-packages (from packaging>20.9->
shap) (3.0.9)
Requirement already satisfied: llvmlite<0.40,>=0.39.0dev0 in
/usr/local/lib/python3.7/dist-packages (from numba->shap)
(0.39.1)
Requirement already satisfied: setuptools<60 in /usr/local/lib/
python3.7/dist-packages (from numba->shap) (57.4.0)
Requirement already satisfied: importlib-metadata in /usr/
local/lib/python3.7/dist-packages (from numba->shap) (4.12.0)
Requirement already satisfied: typing-extensions>=3.6.4 in /
usr/local/lib/python3.7/dist-packages (from importlib-metadata->
numba->shap) (4.1.1)
Requirement already satisfied: zipp>=0.5 in /usr/local/lib/
python3.7/dist-packages (from importlib-metadata->numba->
shap) (3.8.1)
Requirement already satisfied: python-dateutil>=2.7.3 in /usr/
local/lib/python3.7/dist-packages (from pandas->shap) (2.8.2)
Requirement already satisfied: pytz>=2017.3 in /usr/local/lib/
python3.7/dist-packages (from pandas->shap) (2022.2.1)
Requirement already satisfied: six>=1.5 in /usr/local/lib/
python3.7/dist-packages (from python-dateutil>=2.7.3->pandas->
shap) (1.15.0)
Requirement already satisfied: threadpoolctl>=2.0.0 in /usr/
local/lib/python3.7/dist-packages (from scikit-learn->
shap) (3.1.0)
Requirement already satisfied: joblib>=0.11 in /usr/local/lib/
python3.7/dist-packages (from scikit-learn->shap) (1.1.0)
Installing collected packages: slicer, shap
Successfully installed shap-0.41.0 slicer-0.0.7
```

Recipe 1-2. LIME Installation

Problem

You want to install the LIME Python library.

Solution

You can install the LIME library using pip or conda.

How It Works

Let's take a look at the following example script:

```
pip install lime
```

or

```
conda install -c conda-forge lime
```

```
Looking in indexes: https://pypi.org/simple, https://us-python.
pkg.dev/colab-wheels/public/simple/
Collecting lime
  Downloading lime-0.2.0.1.tar.gz (275 kB)
     |████████████████████████████████████████|
     |████████████████████████████| 275 kB 7.5 MB/s
Requirement already satisfied: matplotlib in /usr/local/lib/
python3.7/dist-packages (from lime) (3.2.2)
Requirement already satisfied: numpy in /usr/local/lib/
python3.7/dist-packages (from lime) (1.21.6)
Requirement already satisfied: scipy in /usr/local/lib/
python3.7/dist-packages (from lime) (1.7.3)
Requirement already satisfied: tqdm in /usr/local/lib/
python3.7/dist-packages (from lime) (4.64.1)
```

```
Requirement already satisfied: scikit-learn>=0.18 in /usr/
local/lib/python3.7/dist-packages (from lime) (1.0.2)
Requirement already satisfied: scikit-image>=0.12 in /usr/
local/lib/python3.7/dist-packages (from lime) (0.18.3)
Requirement already satisfied: networkx>=2.0 in /usr/local/lib/
python3.7/dist-packages (from scikit-image>=0.12->lime) (2.6.3)
Requirement already satisfied: PyWavelets>=1.1.1 in /usr/local/
lib/python3.7/dist-packages (from scikit-image>=0.12->
lime) (1.3.0)
Requirement already satisfied: pillow!=7.1.0,!=7.1.1,>=4.3.0 in
/usr/local/lib/python3.7/dist-packages (from scikit-
image>=0.12->lime) (7.1.2)
Requirement already satisfied: imageio>=2.3.0 in /usr/local/
lib/python3.7/dist-packages (from scikit-image>=0.12->
lime) (2.9.0)
Requirement already satisfied: tifffile>=2019.7.26 in /usr/
local/lib/python3.7/dist-packages (from scikit-image>=0.12->
lime) (2021.11.2)
Requirement already satisfied: kiwisolver>=1.0.1 in /usr/local/
lib/python3.7/dist-packages (from matplotlib->lime) (1.4.4)
Requirement already satisfied: cycler>=0.10 in /usr/local/lib/
python3.7/dist-packages (from matplotlib->lime) (0.11.0)
Requirement already satisfied: python-dateutil>=2.1 in /usr/
local/lib/python3.7/dist-packages (from matplotlib->
lime) (2.8.2)
Requirement already satisfied:
pyparsing!=2.0.4,!=2.1.2,!=2.1.6,>=2.0.1 in /usr/local/lib/
python3.7/dist-packages (from matplotlib->lime) (3.0.9)
Requirement already satisfied: typing-extensions in /usr/local/
lib/python3.7/dist-packages (from kiwisolver>=1.0.1->
matplotlib->lime) (4.1.1)
```

Requirement already satisfied: six>=1.5 in /usr/local/lib/
python3.7/dist-packages (from python-dateutil>=2.1->matplotlib->
lime) (1.15.0)
Requirement already satisfied: threadpoolctl>=2.0.0 in /usr/
local/lib/python3.7/dist-packages (from scikit-learn>=0.18->
lime) (3.1.0)
Requirement already satisfied: joblib>=0.11 in /usr/local/lib/
python3.7/dist-packages (from scikit-learn>=0.18->lime) (1.1.0)
Building wheels for collected packages: lime
  Building wheel for lime (setup.py) ... done
  Created wheel for lime: filename=lime-0.2.0.1-py3-none-any.
  whl size=283857 sha256=674ceb94cdcb54588f66c5d5bef5f6ae0326c7
  6e645c40190408791cbe4311d5
  Stored in directory: /root/.cache/pip/wheels/ca/cb/e5/
  ac701e12d365a08917bf4c6171c0961bc880a8181359c66aa7
Successfully built lime
Installing collected packages: lime
Successfully installed lime-0.2.0.1

Recipe 1-3. SHAPASH Installation

Problem

You want to install SHAPASH.

Solution

If you want to use a combination of functions from both the LIME library
and the SHAP library, then you can use the SHAPASH library. You just have
to install it, which is simple.

How It Works

Let's take a look at the following code to install SHAPASH. This is not
available on the Anaconda distribution; the only way to install it is by
using pip.

```
pip install shapash
```

Recipe 1-4. ELI5 Installation

Problem

You want to install ELI5.

Solution

Since this is a Python library, you can use pip.

How It Works

Let's take a look at the following script:

```
pip install eli5
Looking in indexes: https://pypi.org/simple, https://us-python.
pkg.dev/colab-wheels/public/simple/
Collecting eli5
  Downloading eli5-0.13.0.tar.gz (216 kB)
     |████████████████████████████████|
     |████████████████████████████████| 216 kB 6.9 MB/s
Requirement already satisfied: attrs>17.1.0 in /usr/local/lib/
python3.7/dist-packages (from eli5) (22.1.0)
Collecting jinja2>=3.0.0
```

Downloading Jinja2-3.1.2-py3-none-any.whl (133 kB)

███

████████████████████████████| 133 kB 42.7 MB/s
Requirement already satisfied: numpy>=1.9.0 in /usr/local/lib/
python3.7/dist-packages (from eli5) (1.21.6)
Requirement already satisfied: scipy in /usr/local/lib/
python3.7/dist-packages (from eli5) (1.7.3)
Requirement already satisfied: six in /usr/local/lib/python3.7/
dist-packages (from eli5) (1.15.0)
Requirement already satisfied: scikit-learn>=0.20 in /usr/
local/lib/python3.7/dist-packages (from eli5) (1.0.2)
Requirement already satisfied: graphviz in /usr/local/lib/
python3.7/dist-packages (from eli5) (0.10.1)
Requirement already satisfied: tabulate>=0.7.7 in /usr/local/
lib/python3.7/dist-packages (from eli5) (0.8.10)
Requirement already satisfied: MarkupSafe>=2.0 in /usr/local/
lib/python3.7/dist-packages (from jinja2>=3.0.0->eli5) (2.0.1)
Requirement already satisfied: joblib>=0.11 in /usr/local/lib/
python3.7/dist-packages (from scikit-learn>=0.20->eli5) (1.1.0)
Requirement already satisfied: threadpoolctl>=2.0.0 in /usr/
local/lib/python3.7/dist-packages (from scikit-learn>=0.20->
eli5) (3.1.0)
Building wheels for collected packages: eli5
  Building wheel for eli5 (setup.py) ... done
  Created wheel for eli5: filename=eli5-0.13.0-py2.py3-none-
  any.whl size=107748 sha256=3e02d416bd1cc21aebce60420712991
  9a096a92128d7d27c50be1f3a97d3b1de
  Stored in directory: /root/.cache/pip/wheels/cc/3c/96/3ead31a
  8e6c20fc0f1a707fde2e05d49a80b1b4b30096573be
Successfully built eli5
Installing collected packages: jinja2, eli5

```
Attempting uninstall: jinja2
  Found existing installation: Jinja2 2.11.3
  Uninstalling Jinja2-2.11.3:
    Successfully uninstalled Jinja2-2.11.3
ERROR: pip's dependency resolver does not currently take into
account all the packages that are installed. This behavior is
the source of the following dependency conflicts.
flask 1.1.4 requires Jinja2<3.0,>=2.10.1, but you have jinja2
3.1.2 which is incompatible.
Successfully installed eli5-0.13.0 jinja2-3.1.2
```

Recipe 1-5. Skater Installation

Problem

You want to install Skater.

Solution

Skater is an open-source framework to enable model interpretation for
various kinds of machine learning models. The Python-based Skater
library provides both global and local interpretations and can be installed
using pip.

How It Works

Let's take a look at the following script:

```
pip install skater
```

Recipe 1-6. Skope-rules Installation

Problem

You want to install Skopes-rule.

Solution

Skope-rules offers a trade-off between the interpretability of a decision tree and the modeling power of a random forest model. The solution is simple; you use the pip command.

How It Works

Let's take a look at the following code:

```
pip install skope-rules
Looking in indexes: https://pypi.org/simple, https://us-python.
pkg.dev/colab-wheels/public/simple/
Collecting skope-rules
  Downloading skope_rules-1.0.1-py3-none-any.whl (14 kB)
Requirement already satisfied: numpy>=1.10.4 in /usr/local/lib/
python3.7/dist-packages (from skope-rules) (1.21.6)
Requirement already satisfied: scikit-learn>=0.17.1 in /usr/
local/lib/python3.7/dist-packages (from skope-rules) (1.0.2)
Requirement already satisfied: pandas>=0.18.1 in /usr/local/
lib/python3.7/dist-packages (from skope-rules) (1.3.5)
Requirement already satisfied: scipy>=0.17.0 in /usr/local/lib/
python3.7/dist-packages (from skope-rules) (1.7.3)
Requirement already satisfied: pytz>=2017.3 in /usr/local/lib/
python3.7/dist-packages (from pandas>=0.18.1->skope-rules)
(2022.2.1)
```

```
Requirement already satisfied: python-dateutil>=2.7.3 in /usr/
local/lib/python3.7/dist-packages (from pandas>=0.18.1->skope-
rules) (2.8.2)
Requirement already satisfied: six>=1.5 in /usr/local/lib/
python3.7/dist-packages (from python-dateutil>=2.7.3->
pandas>=0.18.1->skope-rules) (1.15.0)
Requirement already satisfied: threadpoolctl>=2.0.0 in /usr/
local/lib/python3.7/dist-packages (from scikit-learn>=0.17.1->
skope-rules) (3.1.0)
Requirement already satisfied: joblib>=0.11 in /usr/local/lib/
python3.7/dist-packages (from scikit-learn>=0.17.1->skope-
rules) (0.11)
Installing collected packages: skope-rules
Successfully installed skope-rules-1.0.1
```

Recipe 1-7. Methods of Model Explainability
Problem

There are various libraries and many explanations for how to identify the
right method for model explainability.

Solution

The explainability method depends on who is the consumer of the model
output, if it is the business or senior management then the explainability
should be very simple and plain English without any mathematical
formula and if the consumer of explainability is data scientists and
machine learning engineers then the explanations may include the
mathematical formulas.

How It Works

The levels of transparency of the machine learning models can be categorized into three buckets, as shown in Figure 1-2.

Methods of Explainability	Textual Explainability	Natural Language Generation
		Summary Generation
	Visual Explainability	Tree based Flow chart
		Rule Extraction
	Example Based	Using common examples
		Business Scenarios

Figure 1-2. *Methods of model explainability*

Textual explanations require explaining the mathematical formula in plain English, which can help business users or senior management. The interpretations can be designed based on model type and model variant and can draw inferences from the model outcome. A template to draw inferences can be designed and mapped to the model types, and then the templates can be filled in using some natural language processing methods.

A visual explainability method can be used to generate charts, graphs such as dendrograms, or any other types of graphs that best explain the relationships. The tree-based methods use `if-else` conditions on the back end; hence, it is simple to show the causality and the relationship.

Using common examples and business scenarios from day-to-day operations and drawing parallels between them can also be useful.

Which method you should choose depends on the problem that needs to be solved and the consumer of the solution where the machine learning model is being used.

Conclusion

In various AI projects and initiatives, the machine learning models generate predictions. Usually, to trust the outcomes of a model, a detailed explanation is required. Since many people are not comfortable explaining the machine learning model outcomes, they cannot reason out the decisions of a model, and thereby AI adoption is restricted. Explainability is required from regulatory stand point as well as auditing and compliance point of view. In high-risk use cases such as medical imaging and object detection or pattern recognition, financial prediction and fraud detection, etc., explainability is required to explain the decisions of the machine learning model.

In this chapter, we set up the environment by installing various explainable AI libraries. Machine learning model interpretability and explainability are the key focuses of this book. We are going to use Python-based libraries, frameworks, methods, classes, and functions to explain the models.

In the next chapter, we are going to look at the linear models.

CHAPTER 2

Explainability for Linear Supervised Models

A supervised learning model is a model that is used to train an algorithm to map input data to output data. A supervised learning model can be of two types: regression or classification. In a regression scenario, the output variable is numerical, whereas with classification, the output variable is binary or multinomial. A binary output variable has two outcomes, such as true and false, accept and reject, yes and no, etc. In the case of multinomial output variables, the outcome can be more than two, such as high, medium, and low. In this chapter, we are going to use explainable libraries to explain a regression model and a classification model, while training a linear model.

In the classical predictive modeling scenario, a function has been identified, and the input data is usually fit to the function to produce the output, where the function is usually predetermined. In a modern predictive modeling scenario, the input data and output are both shown to a group of functions, and the machine identifies the best function that approximates well to the output given a particular set of input. There is a need to explain the output of machine learning and deep learning models when performing regression and classification tasks. Linear regression and linear classification models are simpler to explain.

© Pradeepta Mishra 2023
P. Mishra, *Explainable AI Recipes*, https://doi.org/10.1007/978-1-4842-9029-3_2

The goal of this chapter is to introduce various explainability libraries for linear models such as feature importance, partial dependency plot, and local interpretation.

Recipe 2-1. SHAP Values for a Regression Model on All Numerical Input Variables

Problem

You want to explain a regression model built on all the numeric features of a dataset.

Solution

A regression model on all the numeric features is trained, and then the trained model will be passed through SHAP to generate global explanations and local explanations.

How It Works

Let's take a look at the following script. The Shapely value can be called the SHAP value. It is used to explain the model. It uses the impartial distribution of predictions from a cooperative game theory to attribute a feature to the model's predictions. Input features from the dataset are considered as players in the game. The models function is considered the rules of the game. The Shapely value of a feature is computed based on the following steps:

1. SHAP requires model retraining on all feature subsets; hence, usually it takes time if the explanation has to be generated for larger datasets.

2. Identify a feature set from a list of features (let's say there are 15 features, and we can select a subset with 5 features).

3. For any particular feature, two models using the subset of features will be created, one with the feature and another without the feature.

4. Then the prediction differences will be computed.

5. The differences in prediction are computed for all possible subsets of features.

6. The weighted average value of all possible differences is used to populate the feature importance.

If the weight of the feature is 0.000, then we can conclude that the feature is not important and has not joined the model. If it is not equal to 0.000, then we can conclude that the feature has a role to play in the prediction process.

We are going to use a dataset from the UCI machine learning repository. The URL to access the dataset is as follows:

`https://archive.ics.uci.edu/ml/datasets/Appliances+energy+prediction`

The objective is to predict the appliances' energy use in Wh, using the features from sensors. There are 27 features in the dataset, and here we are trying to understand what features are important in predicting the energy usage. See Table 2-1.

Table 2-1. *Feature Description from the Energy Prediction Dataset*

Feature Name	Description	Unit
Appliances	Energy use	In Wh
Lights	Energy use of light fixtures in the house	In Wh
T1	Temperature in kitchen area	In Celsius
RH_1	Humidity in kitchen area	In %
T2	Temperature in living room area	In Celsius
RH_2	Humidity in living room area	In %
T3	Temperature in laundry room area	
RH_3	Humidity in laundry room area	In %
T4	Temperature in office room	In Celsius
RH_4	Humidity in office room	In %
T5	Temperature in bathroom	In Celsius
RH_5	Humidity in bathroom	In %
T6	Temperature outside the building (north side)	In Celsius
RH_6	Humidity outside the building (north side)	In %
T7	Temperature in ironing room	In Celsius
RH_7	Humidity in ironing room	In %
T8	Temperature in teenager room 2	In Celsius
RH_8	Humidity in teenager room 2	In %
T9	Temperature in parents room	In Celsius
RH_9	Humidity in parents room	In %

(*continued*)

Table 2-1. (*continued*)

Feature Name	Description	Unit
To	Temperature outside (from the Chievres weather station)	In Celsius
Pressure (from Chievres weather station)		In mm Hg
aRH_out	Humidity outside (from the Chievres weather station)	In %
Wind speed (from Chievres weather station)		In m/s
Visibility (from Chievres weather station)		In km
Tdewpoint (from Chievres weather station)		Â°C
rv1	Random variable 1	Nondimensional
rv2	Random variable 2	Nondimensional

```
import pandas as pd
df_lin_reg = pd.read_csv('https://archive.ics.uci.edu/ml/
machine-learning-databases/00374/energydata_complete.csv')
del df_lin_reg['date']
df_lin_reg.info()
df_lin_reg.columns
Index(['Appliances', 'lights', 'T1', 'RH_1', 'T2', 'RH_2',
'T3', 'RH_3', 'T4', 'RH_4', 'T5', 'RH_5', 'T6', 'RH_6', 'T7',
'RH_7', 'T8', 'RH_8', 'T9', 'RH_9', 'T_out', 'Press_mm_hg',
'RH_out', 'Windspeed', 'Visibility', 'Tdewpoint', 'rv1',
'rv2'], dtype='object')
```

```python
#y is the dependent variable, that we need to predict
y = df_lin_reg.pop('Appliances')
# X is the set of input features
X = df_lin_reg

import pandas as pd
import shap
import sklearn

# a simple linear model initialized
model = sklearn.linear_model.LinearRegression()

# linear regression model trained
model.fit(X, y)

print("Model coefficients:\n")
for i in range(X.shape[1]):
    print(X.columns[i], "=", model.coef_[i].round(5))
```

```
Model coefficients:

lights = 1.98971
T1 = -0.60374
RH_1 = 15.15362
T2 = -17.70602
RH_2 = -13.48062
T3 = 25.4064
RH_3 = 4.92457
T4 = -3.46525
RH_4 = -0.17891
T5 = -0.02784
RH_5 = 0.14096
T6 = 7.12616
RH_6 = 0.28795
```

```
T7 = 1.79463
RH_7 = -1.54968
T8 = 8.14656
RH_8 = -4.66968
T9 = -15.87243
RH_9 = -0.90102
T_out = -10.22819
Press_mm_hg = 0.13986
RH_out = -1.06375
Windspeed = 1.70364
Visibility = 0.15368
Tdewpoint = 5.0488
rv1 = -0.02078
rv2 = -0.02078
```

```
# compute the SHAP values for the linear model
explainer = shap.Explainer(model.predict, X)
```

```
# SHAP value calculation
shap_values = explainer(X)
Permutation explainer: 19736it [16:15, 20.08it/s]
```

This part of the script takes time as it is a computationally intensive process. The explainer function calculates permutations, which means taking a feature set and generating the prediction difference. This difference is the presence of one feature and the absence of the same feature. For faster calculation, we can reduce the sample size to a smaller set, let's say 1,000 or 2,000. In the previous script, we are using the entire population of 19,735 records to calculate the SHAP values. This part of the script can be improved by applying Python multiprocessing, which is beyond the scope of this chapter.

The SHAP value for a specific feature i is just the difference between the expected model output and the partial dependence plot at the feature's value xi. One of the fundamental properties of Shapley values is that they always sum up to the difference between the game outcome when all players are present and the game outcome when no players are present. For machine learning models, this means that SHAP values of all the input features will always sum up to the difference between the baseline (expected) model output and the current model output for the prediction being explained.

SHAP values have three objects: (a) the SHAP value for each feature, (b) the base value, and (c) the original training data. As there are 27 features, we can expect 27 shap values.

```
pd.DataFrame(np.round(shap_values.values,3)).head(3)
```

	0	1	2	3	4	5	6	7	8	9	...	17	18	19	20	21	22	23	24	25	26
0	51.732	1.226	106.376	25.393	-54.975	-72.071	28.015	8.056	-1.153	0.077	...	45.453	-3.747	16.410	-3.192	-13.351	4.970	4.077	3.832	0.246	0.246
1	51.732	1.226	92.687	25.393	-54.065	-72.071	28.311	8.056	-1.229	0.077	...	44.924	-3.774	17.603	-3.178	-13.351	4.402	3.488	3.327	0.135	0.135
2	51.732	1.226	86.727	25.393	-52.773	-72.071	29.017	8.311	-1.211	0.077	...	45.982	-3.720	18.797	-3.164	-13.351	3.834	2.898	2.822	-0.074	-0.074

3 rows × 27 columns

```
# average prediction value is called as the base value
pd.DataFrame(np.round(shap_values.base_values,3)).head(3)
```

	0
0	97.494
1	97.494
2	97.494

```
pd.DataFrame(np.round(shap_values.data,3)).head(3)
```

	0	1	2	3	4	5	6	7	8	9	...	17	18	19	20	21	22	23	24	25	26
0	30.0	19.89	47.597	19.2	44.790	19.79	44.730	19.000	45.567	17.167	...	17.033	45.53	6.600	733.5	92.0	7.000	63.000	5.3	13.275	13.275
1	30.0	19.89	46.693	19.2	44.722	19.79	44.790	19.000	45.992	17.167	...	17.067	45.56	6.483	733.6	92.0	6.667	59.167	5.2	18.606	18.606
2	30.0	19.89	46.300	19.2	44.627	19.79	44.933	18.927	45.890	17.167	...	17.000	45.50	6.367	733.7	92.0	6.333	55.333	5.1	28.643	28.643

3 rows × 27 columns

Recipe 2-2. SHAP Partial Dependency Plot for a Regression Model

Problem

You want to get a partial dependency plot from SHAP.

Solution

The solution to this problem is to use the partial dependency method (partial_dependence_plot) from the model.

How It Works

Let's take a look at the following example. There are two ways to get the partial dependency plot, one with a particular data point superimposed and the other without any reference to the data point. See Figure 2-1.

```
# make a standard partial dependence plot for lights on
predicted output for row number 20 from the training dataset.
sample_ind = 20
shap.partial_dependence_plot(
    "lights", model.predict, X, model_expected_value=True,
    feature_expected_value=True, ice=False,
    shap_values=shap_values[sample_ind:sample_ind+1,:]
)
```

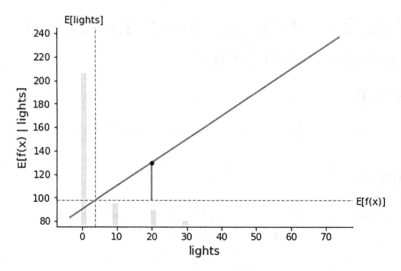

Figure 2-1. *Correlation between feature light and predicted output of the model*

The partial dependency plot is a way to explain the individual predictions and generate local interpretations for the sample selected from the dataset; in this case, the sample 20th record is selected from the training dataset. Figure 2-1 shows the partial dependency superimposed with the 20th record in red.

```
shap.partial_dependence_plot(
    "lights", model.predict, X, ice=False,
    model_expected_value=True, feature_expected_value=True
)
```

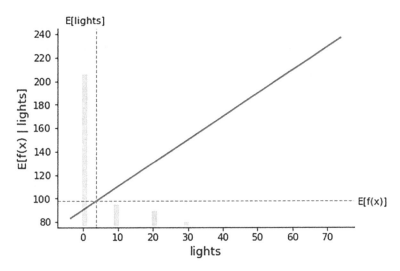

Figure 2-2. *Partial dependency plot between lights and predicted outcome from the model*

```
# the waterfall_plot shows how we get from shap_values.base_
values to model.predict(X)[sample_ind]
shap.plots.waterfall(shap_values[sample_ind], max_display=14)
```

27

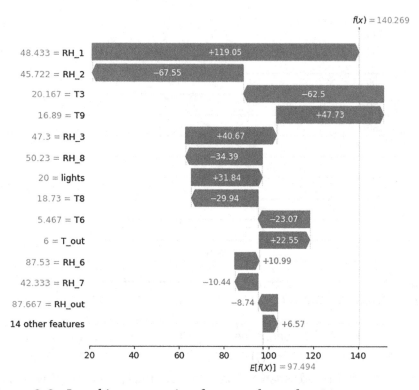

Figure 2-3. *Local interpretation for record number 20*

The local interpretation for record number 20 from the training dataset is displayed in Figure 2-3. The predicted output for the 20th record is 140 Wh. The most influential feature impacting the 20th record is RH_1, which is the humidity in the kitchen area in percentage, and RH_2, which is the humidity in the living room area. On the bottom of Figure 2-3, there are 14 features that are not very important for the 20th record's predicted value.

```
X[20:21]
model.predict(X[20:21])
array([140.26911466])
```

Recipe 2-3. SHAP Feature Importance for Regression Model with All Numerical Input Variables

Problem

You want to calculate the feature importance using the SHAP values.

Solution

The solution to this problem is to use SHAP absolute values from the model.

How It Works

Let's take a look at the following example. SHAP values can be used to show the global importance of features. Importance features means features that have a larger importance in predicting the output.

```
#computing shap importance values for the linear model
import numpy as np
feature_names = shap_values.feature_names
shap_df = pd.DataFrame(shap_values.values,
columns=feature_names)
vals = np.abs(shap_df.values).mean(0)
shap_importance = pd.DataFrame(list(zip(feature_names, vals)),
columns=['col_name', 'feature_importance_vals'])
shap_importance.sort_values(by=['feature_importance_vals'],
ascending=False, inplace=True)
```

```
print(shap_importance)
         col_name  feature_importance_vals
2            RH_1                 49.530061
19          T_out                 43.828847
4            RH_2                 42.911069
5              T3                 41.671587
11             T6                 34.653893
3              T2                 31.097282
17             T9                 26.607721
16           RH_8                 19.920029
24       Tdewpoint               17.443688
21         RH_out                13.044643
6            RH_3                 13.042064
15             T8                 12.803450
0            lights                11.907603
12           RH_6                  7.806188
14           RH_7                  6.578015
7              T4                  5.866801
22       Windspeed                3.361895
13             T7                  3.182072
18           RH_9                  3.041144
23       Visibility               1.385616
10           RH_5                  0.855398
20       Press_mm_hg              0.823456
1              T1                  0.765753
8            RH_4                  0.642723
25             rv1                 0.260885
26             rv2                 0.260885
9              T5                  0.041905
```

All the feature importance values are not scaled; hence, sum of values from all features will not be totaling 100.

The beeswarm chart in Figure 2-4 shows the impact of SHAP values on model output. The blue dot shows a low feature value, and a red dot shows a high feature value. Each dot indicates one data point from the dataset. The beeswarm plot shows the distribution of feature values against the SHAP values.

```
shap.plots.beeswarm(shap_values)
```

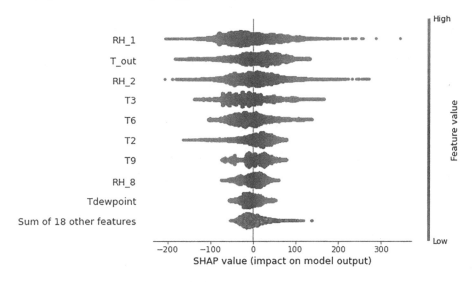

Figure 2-4. *Impact on model output*

Recipe 2-4. SHAP Values for a Regression Model on All Mixed Input Variables

Problem

How do you estimate SHAP values when you introduce the categorical variables along with the numerical variables, which is a mixed set of input features.

Solution

The solution is that the mixed input variables that have numeric features as well as categorical or binary features can be modeled together. As the number of features increases, the time to compute all the permutations will also increase.

How It Works

We are going to use an automobile public dataset with some modifications. The objective is to predict the price of a vehicle given the features such as make, location, age, etc. It is a regression problem that we are going to solve using a mix of numeric and categorical features.

```
df = pd.read_csv('https://raw.githubusercontent.com/
pradmishra1/PublicDatasets/main/automobile.csv')
df.head(3)
df.columns
Index(['Price', 'Make', 'Location', 'Age', 'Odometer',
'FuelType', 'Transmission', 'OwnerType', 'Mileage', 'EngineCC',
'PowerBhp'], dtype='object')
```

We cannot use string-based features or categorical features in the model directly as matrix multiplication is not possible on string features; hence, the string-based features need to be transformed into dummy variables or binary features with 0 and 1 flags. The transformation step is skipped here because many data scientists already know how to do this data transformation. We are importing another transformed dataset directly.

```
df_t = pd.read_csv('https://raw.githubusercontent.com/
pradmishra1/PublicDatasets/main/Automobile_transformed.csv')
del df_t['Unnamed: 0']
```

```
df_t.head(3)
df_t.columns
Index(['Price', 'Age', 'Odometer', 'mileage', 'engineCC',
'powerBhp', 'Location_Bangalore', 'Location_Chennai',
'Location_Coimbatore', 'Location_Delhi', 'Location_Hyderabad',
'Location_Jaipur', 'Location_Kochi', 'Location_Kolkata',
'Location_Mumbai', 'Location_Pune', 'FuelType_Diesel',
'FuelType_Electric', 'FuelType_LPG', 'FuelType_Petrol',
'Transmission_Manual', 'OwnerType_Fourth +ACY- Above',
'OwnerType_Second', 'OwnerType_Third'], dtype='object')

#y is the dependent variable, that we need to predict
y = df_t.pop('Price')
# X is the set of input features
X = df_t

import pandas as pd
import shap
import sklearn

# a simple linear model initialized
model = sklearn.linear_model.LinearRegression()

# linear regression model trained
model.fit(X, y)

print("Model coefficients:\n")
for i in range(X.shape[1]):
    print(X.columns[i], "=", model.coef_[i].round(5))
Model coefficients:

Age = -0.92281
Odometer = 0.0
mileage = -0.07923
engineCC = -4e-05
```

```
powerBhp = 0.1356
Location_Bangalore = 2.00658
Location_Chennai = 0.94944
Location_Coimbatore = 2.23592
Location_Delhi = -0.29837
Location_Hyderabad = 1.8771
Location_Jaipur = 0.8738
Location_Kochi = 0.03311
Location_Kolkata = -0.86024
Location_Mumbai = -0.81593
Location_Pune = 0.33843
FuelType_Diesel = -1.2545
FuelType_Electric = 7.03139
FuelType_LPG = 0.79077
FuelType_Petrol = -2.8691
Transmission_Manual = -2.92415
OwnerType_Fourth +ACY- Above = 1.7104
OwnerType_Second = -0.55923
OwnerType_Third = 0.76687
```

To compute the SHAP values, we can use the explainer function with the training dataset X and model predict function. The SHAP value calculation happens using a permutation approach; it took 5 minutes.

```
# compute the SHAP values for the linear model
explainer = shap.Explainer(model.predict, X)

# SHAP value calculation
shap_values = explainer(X)
Permutation explainer: 6020it [05:14, 18.59it/s]
```

```
import numpy as np
pd.DataFrame(np.round(shap_values.values,3)).head(3)
```

	0	1	2	3	4	5	6	7	8	9	...	13	14	15	16	17	18	19	20	21	22
0	-3.700	0.006	-0.738	0.031	-9.077	-0.04	-0.066	-0.246	0.027	-0.225	...	-0.653	-0.020	0.765	0.0	0.0	1.119	-0.965	0.0	0.095	-0.008
1	0.914	-0.006	-0.188	0.009	0.149	-0.04	-0.066	-0.246	0.027	-0.225	...	0.163	0.318	-0.489	0.0	0.0	1.119	-0.965	0.0	0.095	-0.008
2	-2.778	-0.004	-0.072	0.023	-4.936	-0.04	0.883	-0.246	0.027	-0.225	...	0.163	-0.020	0.765	0.0	0.0	-1.750	-0.965	0.0	0.095	-0.008

3 rows × 23 columns

```
# average prediction value is called as the base value
pd.DataFrame(np.round(shap_values.base_values,3)).head(3)
```

	0 .
0	11.933
1	11.933
2	11.933

```
pd.DataFrame(np.round(shap_values.data,3)).head(3)
```

	0	1	2	3	4	5	6	7	8	9	...	13	14	15	16	17	18	19	20	21	22
0	10.0	72000.0	26.60	998.0	58.16	0.0	0.0	0.0	0.0	0.0	...	1.0	0.0	0.0	0.0	0.0	0.0	1.0	0.0	0.0	0.0
1	5.0	41000.0	19.67	1582.0	126.20	0.0	0.0	0.0	0.0	0.0	...	0.0	1.0	1.0	0.0	0.0	0.0	1.0	0.0	0.0	0.0
2	9.0	46000.0	18.20	1199.0	88.70	0.0	1.0	0.0	0.0	0.0	...	0.0	0.0	0.0	0.0	0.0	1.0	1.0	0.0	0.0	0.0

3 rows × 23 columns

Recipe 2-5. SHAP Partial Dependency Plot for Regression Model for Mixed Input Problem

You want to plot the partial dependency plot and interpret the graph for numeric and categorical dummy variables.

Solution

The partial dependency plot shows the correlation between the feature and the predicted output of the target variables. There are two ways we can showcase the results, one with a feature and expected value of the prediction function and the other with superimposing a data point on the partial dependency plot.

How It Works

Let's take a look at the following example (see Figure 2-5):

```
shap.partial_dependence_plot(
    "powerBhp", model.predict, X, ice=False,
    model_expected_value=True, feature_expected_value=True
)
```

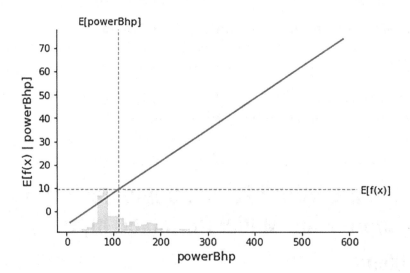

Figure 2-5. *Partial dependency plot for powerBhp and predicted price of the vehicle*

The linear blue line shows the positive correlation between the price and the powerBhp. The powerBhp is a strong feature. The higher the bhp, the higher the price of the car. This is a continuous or numeric feature; let's look at the binary or dummy features. There are two dummy features if the car is registered in a Bangalore location or in a Kolkata location as dummy variables. See Figure 2-6.

```
shap.partial_dependence_plot(
    "Location_Bangalore", model.predict, X, ice=False,
    model_expected_value=True, feature_expected_value=True
)
```

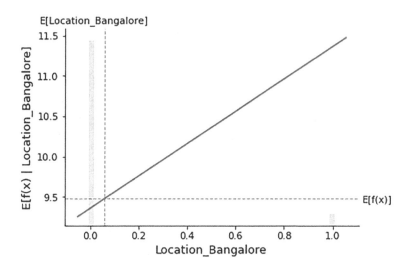

Figure 2-6. *Dummy variable Bangalore location versus SHAP value*

If the location of the car is Bangalore, then the price would be higher, and vice versa. See Figure 2-7.

```
shap.partial_dependence_plot(
    "Location_Kolkata", model.predict, X, ice=False,
    model_expected_value=True, feature_expected_value=True
)
```

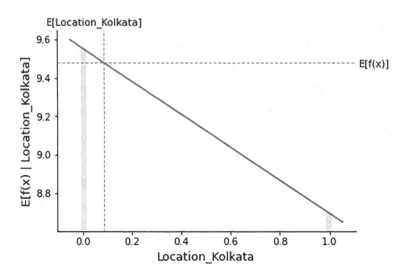

Figure 2-7. *Dummy variable Location_Kolkata versus SHAP value*

If the location is Kolkata, then the price is expected to be lower. The reason for the difference between the two locations is in the data that is being used to train the model. The previous three figures show the global importance of a feature versus the prediction function. As an example, only two features are taken into consideration; we can use all features one by one and display many graphs to get more understanding about the predictions.

Now let's look at a sample data point superimposed on a partial dependence plot to display local explanations. See Figure 2-8.

```
# make a standard partial dependence plot for lights on
predicted output
sample_ind = 20 #20th record from the dataset
shap.partial_dependence_plot(
    "powerBhp", model.predict, X, model_expected_value=True,
    feature_expected_value=True, ice=False,
    shap_values=shap_values[sample_ind:sample_ind+1,:]
)
```

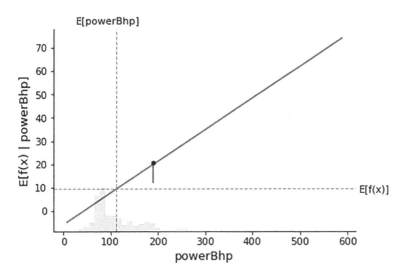

Figure 2-8. *Power bhp versus prediction function*

The vertical dotted line shows the average powerBhp, and the horizontal dotted line shows the average predicted value by the model. The small blue bar dropping from the black dot reflects the placement of record number 20 from the dataset. Local interpretation means that for any sample record from the dataset, we should be able to explain the predictions. Figure 2-9 shows the importance of features corresponding to each record in the dataset.

```
# the waterfall_plot shows how we get from shap_values.base_
values to model.predict(X)[sample_ind]
shap.plots.waterfall(shap_values[sample_ind], max_display=14)
```

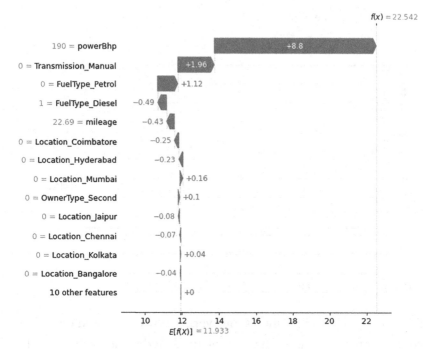

Figure 2-9. *Local interpretation of the 20th record and corresponding feature importance*

For the 20th record, the predicted price is 22.542, the powerBhp stands out to be most important feature, and manual transmission is the second most important feature.

```
X[20:21]
model.predict(X[20:21])
array([22.54213017])
```

Recipe 2-6. SHAP Feature Importance for a Regression Model with All Mixed Input Variables

Problem

You want to get the global feature importance from SHAP values using mixed-input feature data.

Solution

The solution to this problem is to use absolute values and sort them in descending order.

How It Works

Let's take a look at the following example:

```
#computing shap importance values for the linear model
import numpy as np
# feature names from the training data
feature_names = shap_values.feature_names
#combining the shap values with feature names
shap_df = pd.DataFrame(shap_values.values,
columns=feature_names)
#taking the absolute shap values
vals = np.abs(shap_df.values).mean(0)
#creating a dataframe view
shap_importance = pd.DataFrame(list(zip(feature_names, vals)),
columns=['col_name', 'feature_importance_vals'])
#sorting the importance values
```

```
shap_importance.sort_values(by=['feature_importance_vals'],
ascending=False, inplace=True)
print(shap_importance)
```

col_name	feature_importance_vals	
4	powerBhp	6.057831
0	Age	2.338342
18	FuelType_Petrol	1.406920
19	Transmission_Manual	1.249077
15	FuelType_Diesel	0.618288
7	Location_Coimbatore	0.430233
9	Location_Hyderabad	0.401118
2	mileage	0.270872
13	Location_Mumbai	0.227442
5	Location_Bangalore	0.154706
21	OwnerType_Second	0.154429
6	Location_Chennai	0.133476
10	Location_Jaipur	0.127807
12	Location_Kolkata	0.111829
14	Location_Pune	0.051082
8	Location_Delhi	0.049372
22	OwnerType_Third	0.021778
3	engineCC	0.020145
1	Odometer	0.009602
11	Location_Kochi	0.007474
20	OwnerType_Fourth +ACY- Above	0.002557
16	FuelType_Electric	0.002336
17	FuelType_LPG	0.001314

At a high level, for the linear model that is used to predict the price of the automobiles, the previous features are important, with the highest being the powerBhp, age of the car, petrol type, manual transmission type, etc. The previous tabular output shows global feature importance.

Recipe 2-7. SHAP Strength for Mixed Features on the Predicted Output for Regression Models

Problem

You want to know the impact of a feature on the model function.

Solution

The solution to this problem is to use a beeswarm plot that displays the blue and red points.

How It Works

Let's take a look at the following example (see Figure 2-10). From the beeswarm plot there is a positive relationship between powerBhp and positive SHAP value; however, there is a negative correlation between the age of a car and the price of the car. As the feature value increases from a lower powerBhp value to a higher powerBhp value, the shap value increases and vice versa. However, there is an opposite trend for the age feature.

```
shap.plots.beeswarm(shap_values)
```

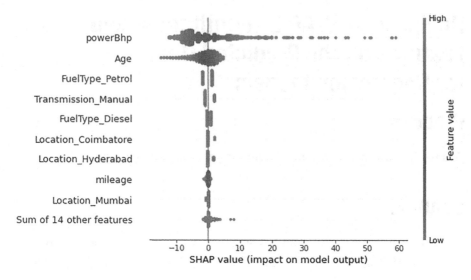

Figure 2-10. *The SHAP value impact on the model output*

Recipe 2-8. SHAP Values for a Regression Model on Scaled Data

Problem

You don't know whether getting SHAP values on scaled data is better than the unscaled numerical data.

Solution

The solution to this problem is to use a numerical dataset and generate local and global explanations after applying the standard scaler to the data.

How It Works

Let's take a look at the following script:

```
import pandas as pd
df_lin_reg = pd.read_csv('https://archive.ics.uci.edu/ml/
machine-learning-databases/00374/energydata_complete.csv')
del df_lin_reg['date']
#y is the dependent variable, that we need to predict
y = df_lin_reg.pop('Appliances')
# X is the set of input features
X = df_lin_reg
import pandas as pd
import shap
import sklearn
#create standardized features
scaler = sklearn.preprocessing.StandardScaler()
scaler.fit(X)
#transform the dataset
X_std = scaler.transform(X)
# a simple linear model initialized
model = sklearn.linear_model.LinearRegression()

# linear regression model trained
model.fit(X_std, y)
print("Model coefficients:\n")
for i in range(X.shape[1]):
    print(X.columns[i], "=", model.coef_[i].round(5))
Model coefficients:
lights = 15.7899
T1 = -0.96962
RH_1 = 60.29926
T2 = -38.82785
```

RH_2 = -54.8622
T3 = 50.96675
RH_3 = 16.02699
T4 = -7.07893
RH_4 = -0.77668
T5 = -0.05136
RH_5 = 1.27172
T6 = 43.3997
RH_6 = 8.96929
T7 = 3.78656
RH_7 = -7.92521
T8 = 15.93559
RH_8 = -24.39546
T9 = -31.97757
RH_9 = -3.74049
T_out = -54.38609
Press_mm_hg = 1.03483
RH_out = -15.85058
Windspeed = 4.17588
Visibility = 1.81258
Tdewpoint = 21.17741
rv1 = -0.30118
rv2 = -0.30118
CodeText

```
# compute the SHAP values for the linear model
explainer = shap.Explainer(model.predict, X_std)

# SHAP value calculation
shap_values = explainer(X_std)

Permutation explainer: 19736it [08:53, 36.22it/s]
```

It is faster to get results from the SHAP explainer because we are using the standardized data. The SHAP values also changed a bit, but there are no major changes to the shap values.

	Permutation explainer	Time
Unscaled data	19736it	15:22, 21.23it/s
Scaled data	19736it	08:53, 36.22it/s

```
#computing shap importance values for the linear model
import numpy as np
# feature names from the training data
feature_names = X.columns
#combining the shap values with feature names
shap_df = pd.DataFrame(shap_values.values,
columns=feature_names)
#taking the absolute shap values
vals = np.abs(shap_df.values).mean(0)
#creating a dataframe view
shap_importance = pd.DataFrame(list(zip(feature_names, vals)),
columns=['col_name', 'feature_importance_vals'])
#sorting the importance values
shap_importance.sort_values(by=['feature_importance_vals'],
ascending=False, inplace=True)

print(shap_importance)
        col_name  feature_importance_vals
2           RH_1                49.530061
19         T_out                43.828847
4           RH_2                42.911069
5             T3                41.671587
11            T6                34.653893
```

3	T2	31.097282
17	T9	26.607721
16	RH_8	19.920029
24	Tdewpoint	17.443688
21	RH_out	13.044643
6	RH_3	13.042064
15	T8	12.803450
0	lights	11.907603
12	RH_6	7.806188
14	RH_7	6.578015
7	T4	5.866801
22	Windspeed	3.361895
13	T7	3.182072
18	RH_9	3.041144
23	Visibility	1.385616
10	RH_5	0.855398
20	Press_mm_hg	0.823456
1	T1	0.765753
8	RH_4	0.642723
25	rv1	0.260885
26	rv2	0.260885
9	T5	0.041905

Recipe 2-9. LIME Explainer for Tabular Data Problem

You want to know how to generate explainability at a local level in a focused manner rather than at a global level.

Solution

The solution to this problem is to use the LIME library. LIME is a model-agnostic technique; it retrains the ML model while running the explainer. LIME localizes a problem and explains the model at a local level.

How It Works

Let's take a look at the following example. LIME requires a numpy array as an input to the tabular explainer; hence, the Pandas dataframe needs to be transformed into an array.

```
!pip install lime
Looking in indexes: https://pypi.org/simple, https://us-python.
pkg.dev/colab-wheels/public/simple/
Collecting lime
  Downloading lime-0.2.0.1.tar.gz (275 kB)
     |████████████████████████████████| 275 kB 3.9 MB/s
Requirement already satisfied: matplotlib in /usr/local/lib/
python3.7/dist-packages (from lime) (3.2.2)
Requirement already satisfied: numpy in /usr/local/lib/
python3.7/dist-packages (from lime) (1.21.6)
Requirement already satisfied: scipy in /usr/local/lib/
python3.7/dist-packages (from lime) (1.7.3)
Require
..............
import lime
import lime.lime_tabular

explainer = lime.lime_tabular.LimeTabularExplainer(np.array(X),
                                      mode='regression',
                                      feature_names=
                                      X.columns,
```

```
                                       class_names=
                                       ['price'],
                                         verbose=True)
```

We are using the energy prediction data from this chapter only.

```
Explainer.feature_selection
# asking for explanation for LIME model
I = 60
exp = explainer.explain_instance(np.array(X)[i],
                                 model.predict,
                                 num_features=14
                                 )

model.predict(X)[60]

X[60:61]
Intercept -142.75931081140854
Prediction_local [-492.87528974]
Right: -585.148657732673
exp.show_in_notebook(show_table=True)
```

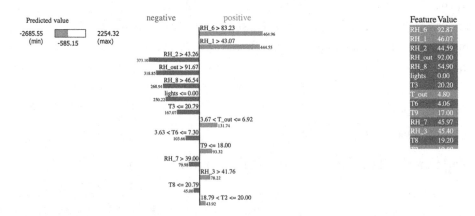

Figure 2-11. *Local explanation for the 60ᵗʰ record from the dataset*

```
exp.as_list()
[('RH_6 > 83.23', 464.95860873125986), ('RH_1 > 43.07',
444.5520820612734), ('RH_2 > 43.26', -373.10130212185885), ('RH_out >
91.67', -318.85242557316906), ('RH_8 > 46.54', -268.93915670002696),
('lights <= 0.00', -250.2220287090558), ('T3 <= 20.79',
-167.06955734678837), ('3.67 < T_out <= 6.92', 131.73980385122888),
('3.63 < T6 <= 7.30', -103.65788170866274), ('T9 <= 18.00',
93.3237211878042), ('RH_7 > 39.00', -79.9838215229673), ('RH_3 >
41.76', 78.2163751694391), ('T8 <= 20.79', -45.00198774806178),
('18.79 < T2 <= 20.00', 43.92159150217912)]
```

Recipe 2-10. ELI5 Explainer for Tabular Data

Problem

You want to use the ELI5 library for generating explanations of a linear regression model.

Solution

ELI5 is a Python package that helps to debug a machine learning model and explain the predictions. It provides support for all machine learning models supported by the scikit-learn library.

How It Works

Let's take a look at the following script:

```
pip install eli5
import eli5
eli5.show_weights(model,
                  feature_names=list(X.columns))
```

y top features

Weight?	Feature
+97.695	<BIAS>
+60.299	RH_1
+50.967	T3
+43.400	T6
+21.177	Tdewpoint
+16.027	RH_3
+15.936	T8
+15.790	Lights
+8.969	RH_6
+4.176	Windspeed
+3.787	T7

... 3 more positive ...

... 5 more negative ...

-3.740	RH_9
-7.079	T4
-7.925	RH_7
-15.851	RH_out
-24.395	RH_8
-31.978	T9
-38.828	T2
-54.386	T_out
-54.862	RH_2

```
eli5.explain_weights(model, feature_names=list(X.columns))
eli5.explain_prediction(model,X.iloc[60])
from eli5.sklearn import PermutationImportance

# a simple linear model initialized
model = sklearn.linear_model.LinearRegression()

# linear regression model trained
model.fit(X, y)
perm = PermutationImportance(model)
perm.fit(X, y)
eli5.show_weights(perm,feature_names=list(X.columns))
```

The results table has a BIAS value as a feature. This can be interpreted as an intercept term for a linear regression model. Other features are listed based on the descending order of importance based on their weight. The show weights function provides a global interpretation of the model, and the show prediction function provides a local interpretation by taking into account a record from the training set.

Recipe 2-11. How the Permutation Model in ELI5 Works

Problem

You want to make sense of the ELI5 permutation library.

Solution

The solution to this problem is to use a dataset and a trained model.

How It Works

The permutation model in the ELI5 library works only for global interpretation. First, it takes a base line linear regression model from the training dataset and computes the error of the model. Then it shuffles the values of a feature and retrains the model and computes the error. It compares the decrease in error after shuffling and before shuffling. A feature can be considered as important if post shuffling the error delta is high and unimportant if the error delta is low. The result displays the average importance of features and the standard deviation of features with multiple shuffle steps.

Recipe 2-12. Global Explanation for Logistic Regression Models

Problem

You want to explain the predictions generated from a logistic regression model.

Solution

The logistic regression model is also known as a classification model as we model the probabilities from either a binary classification or a multinomial classification variable. In this particular recipe, we are using a churn classification dataset that has two outcomes: whether the customer is likely to churn or not.

How It Works

Let's take a look at the following example. The key is to get the SHAP values, which will return base values, SHAP values, and data. Using the SHAP values, we can create various explanations using graphs and figures. The SHAP values are always at a global level.

```
import pandas as pd
import numpy as np
import matplotlib.pyplot as plt
%matplotlib inline
from sklearn.linear_model import LogisticRegression,
LogisticRegressionCV
from sklearn.metrics import confusion_matrix,
classification_report

df_train = pd.read_csv('https://raw.githubusercontent.com/
pradmishra1/PublicDatasets/main/ChurnData_test.csv')
from sklearn.preprocessing import LabelEncoder

tras = LabelEncoder()
df_train['area_code_tr'] = tras.fit_transform(df_
train['area_code'])
df_train.columns
del df_train['area_code']
df_train.columns
df_train['target_churn_dum'] = pd.get_dummies(df_train.
churn,prefix='churn',drop_first=True)
df_train.columns
del df_train['international_plan']
del df_train['voice_mail_plan']
del df_train['churn']
df_train.info()
```

```
del df_train['Unnamed: 0']
df_train.columns
from sklearn.model_selection import train_test_split

df_train.columns

X = df_train[['account_length', 'number_vmail_messages',
'total_day_minutes',
        'total_day_calls', 'total_day_charge', 'total_eve_
        minutes',
        'total_eve_calls', 'total_eve_charge', 'total_night_
        minutes',
        'total_night_calls', 'total_night_charge', 'total_intl_
        minutes',
        'total_intl_calls', 'total_intl_charge',
        'number_customer_service_calls', 'area_code_tr']]
Y = df_train['target_churn_dum']
xtrain,xtest,ytrain,ytest=train_test_split(X,Y,test_
size=0.20,stratify=Y)
log_model = LogisticRegression()

log_model.fit(xtrain,ytrain)

print("training accuracy:", log_model.score(xtrain,ytrain))
#training accuracy

print("test accuracy:",log_model.score(xtest,ytest)) # test
accuracy
# Provide Probability as Output
def model_churn_proba(x):
    return log_model.predict_proba(x)[:,1]
```

```
# Provide Log Odds as Output
def model_churn_log_odds(x):
    p = log_model.predict_log_proba(x)
    return p[:,1] - p[:,0]
# compute the SHAP values for the linear model
background_churn = shap.maskers.Independent(X, max_
samples=2000)
explainer = shap.Explainer(log_model, background_churn,feature_
names=list(X.columns))
shap_values_churn = explainer(X)
shap_values_churn
.values = array([[-5.68387743e-03, 2.59884057e-01,
-1.12707664e+00, ..., 1.70015539e-04, 6.35113804e-01,
-5.98927431e-03], [-9.26328584e-02, 2.59884057e-01,
4.31613190e-01, ..., -4.82342680e-04, -7.11876922e-01,
-5.98927431e-03], [-1.05143764e-02, -8.06452301e-01,
1.15736857e+00, ..., 2.05960486e-03, -2.62880014e-01,
5.88245015e-03], ..., [ 9.09261014e-02, 2.59884057e-01,
-4.15611799e-01, ..., 1.99211953e-03, -2.62880014e-01,
-5.34120777e-05], [-2.50058732e-02, 2.59884057e-01,
7.63911460e-02, ..., -1.08971068e-03, -7.11876922e-01,
-5.98927431e-03], [ 3.05448646e-02, -9.90303397e-01,
-5.29936135e-01, ..., -6.17313346e-04, -7.11876922e-01,
-5.34120777e-05]]) .base_values = array([-2.18079251,
-2.18079251, -2.18079251, ..., -2.18079251, -2.18079251,
-2.18079251]) .data = array([[101. , 0. , 70.9 , ..., 2.86, 3.
, 2. ], [137. , 0. , 223.6 , ..., 2.57, 0. , 2. ], [103. , 29.
, 294.7 , ..., 3.7 , 1. , 0. ], ..., [ 61. , 0. , 140.6 , ...,
3.67, 1. , 1. ], [109. , 0. , 188.8 , ..., 2.3 , 0. , 2. ], [
86. , 34. , 129.4 , ..., 2.51, 0. , 1. ]])
shap_values = pd.DataFrame(shap_values_churn.values)
```

```
shap_values.columns = list(X.columns)
shap_values
```

	account_length	number_vmail_messages	total_day_minutes	total_day_calls	total_day_charge	total_eve_minutes	total_eve_calls	total_eve_charge	total_
0	-0.005684	0.259884	-1.127077	-0.180561	-0.025010	0.018183	0.451987	0.000321	
1	-0.092633	0.259884	0.431613	0.100345	0.009572	0.068239	-0.638957	0.001207	

```
# compute the SHAP values for the linear model
explainer_log_odds = shap.Explainer(log_model, background_
churn,feature_names=list(X.columns))
shap_values_churn_log_odds = explainer_log_odds(X)
shap_values_churn_log_odds
```

Recipe 2-13. Partial Dependency Plot for a Classifier

Problem

You want to show feature associations with the class probabilities.

Solution

The class probabilities in this example are related to predicting the probability of churn. The SHAP value for a feature can be plotted against the feature value to show a scatter chart that displays the correlation (positive or negative) and strength of associations.

How It Works

Let's take a look at the following script:

```
shap.plots.scatter(shap_values_churn[:,'account_length'])
```

The Figure 2-12 shows the relationship between account length variable and the SHAP values of the account length variable.

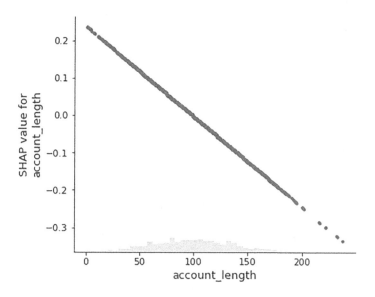

Figure 2-12. *Account length and SHAP value of account length*

```
# make a standard partial dependence plot
sample_ind = 25
fig,ax = shap.partial_dependence_plot(
    "number_vmail_messages", model_churn_proba, X, model_
    expected_value=True,
    feature_expected_value=True, show=False,ice=False)
```

The Figure 2-13 shows the relationship between feature number of voice mail messages and the SHAP value of number of voice mail messages.

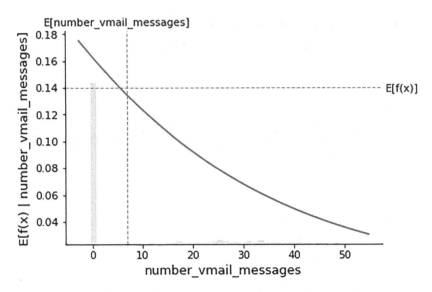

Figure 2-13. *Number of voicemail messages and their shap values*

```
shap.plots.bar(shap_values_churn_log_odds)
```

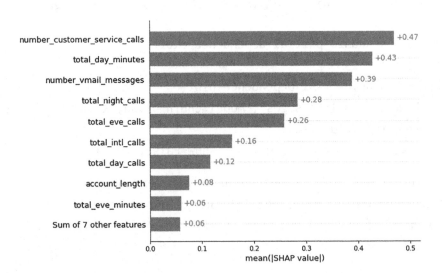

Figure 2-14. *Mean absolute shap values of all features*

Recipe 2-14. Global Feature Importance from the Classifier

Problem

You want to get the global feature importance for the logistic regression model.

Solution

The solution to this problem is to use a bar plot and beeswarm plot and heat map.

How It Works

Let's take a look at the following script (see Figure 2-15 and Figure 2-16):

```
shap.plots.beeswarm(shap_values_churn_log_odds)
```

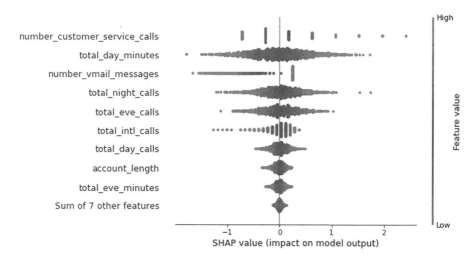

Figure 2-15. *SHAP value impact on the model output*

```
shap.plots.heatmap(shap_values_churn_log_odds[:1000])
```

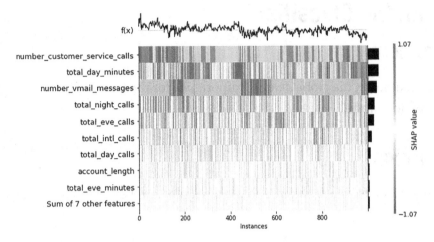

Figure 2-16. *Heat map for SHAP value and positive and negative feature contributions*

```
temp_df = pd.DataFrame()
temp_df['Feature Name'] = pd.Series(X.columns)
temp_df['Coefficients'] = pd.Series(log_model.coef_.flatten())
temp_df.sort_values(by='Coefficients',ascending=False)
```

The interpretation goes like this: when we change the value of a feature by 1 unit, the model equation will produce two odds; one is the base, and the other is the incremental value of the feature. We are looking at the ratio of odds changing with every increase or decrease in the value of a feature. From the global feature importance, there are three important features: the number of customer service calls, the total minutes for the day, and the number of voicemail messages.

Recipe 2-15. Local Explanations Using LIME

Problem

You want to get faster explanations from both global and local explainable libraries.

Solution

The model explanation can be done using SHAP; however, one of the limitations of SHAP is we cannot use the full data to create global and local explanations. Even if we decide to use the full data, it usually takes more time. Hence, LIME is very useful to speed up the process of generating local and global explanations in a scenario when millions of records are being used to train a model.

How It Works

Let's take a look at the following script:

```
import lime
import lime.lime_tabular

explainer = lime.lime_tabular.LimeTabularExplainer(np.
          array(xtrain),
                  feature_names=list(xtrain.columns),
                  class_names=['target_churn_dum'],
                  verbose=True, mode='classification')
# this record is a no churn scenario
exp = explainer.explain_instance(xtest.iloc[0], log_model.
predict_proba, num_features=16)
exp.as_list()
Intercept -0.005325152786766457
```

```
Prediction_local [0.38147987]
Right: 0.32177492114146566
X does not have valid feature names, but LogisticRegression was
fitted with feature names
[('number_customer_service_calls > 2.00', 0.1530891322197175),
 ('total_day_minutes > 213.80', 0.11114575899827552),
 ('number_vmail_messages <= 0.00', 0.09610037835765535),
 ('total_intl_calls <= 3.00', 0.031770167783340472),
 ('total_day_calls <= 86.00', 0.029375047698073507),
 ('99.00 < total_night_calls <= 113.00',
 -0.023964881054121437),
 ('account_length > 126.00', -0.015756474385902122),
 ('88.00 < total_eve_calls <= 101.00', 0.008756083756550214),
 ('total_intl_minutes <= 8.60', -0.007205495334049559),
 ('200.00 < total_eve_minutes <= 232.00',
 0.004122691218360631),
 ('total_intl_charge <= 2.32', -0.0013747713519713068),
 ('total_day_charge > 36.35', 0.0010811737941700244),
 ('200.20 < total_night_minutes <= 234.80',
 -0.00013400510199346275),
 ('0.00 < area_code_tr <= 1.00', -8.127174069198377e-05),
 ('9.01 < total_night_charge <= 10.57',
 -6.668417986225894e-05),
 ('17.00 < total_eve_charge <= 19.72', -5.18320207196282e-05)]
pd.DataFrame(exp.as_list())
```

0	1	
0	number_customer_service_calls > 2.00	0.153089
1	total_day_minutes > 213.80	0.111146
2	number_vmail_messages <= 0.00	0.096100
3	total_intl_calls <= 3.00	0.031770
4	total_day_calls <= 86.00	0.029375
5	99.00 < total_night_calls <= 113.00	-0.023965
6	account_length > 126.00	-0.015756
7	88.00 < total_eve_calls <= 101.00	0.008756
8	total_intl_minutes <= 8.60	-0.007205
9	200.00 < total_eve_minutes <= 232.00	0.004123
10	total_intl_charge <= 2.32	-0.001375
11	total_day_charge > 36.35	0.001081
12	200.20 < total_night_minutes <= 234.80	-0.000134
13	0.00 < area_code_tr <= 1.00	-0.000081
14	9.01 < total_night_charge <= 10.57	-0.000067

```
exp.show_in_notebook(show_table=True)
```

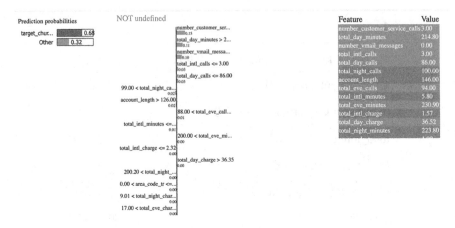

Figure 2-17.   *Local explanation for record number 1*

```
# This is s churn scenario
exp = explainer.explain_instance(xtest.iloc[20], log_model.
predict_proba, num_features=16)
exp.as_list()
ntercept -0.02171544428872446
Prediction_local [0.44363396]
Right: 0.4309152994720991
X does not have valid feature names, but LogisticRegression was
fitted with feature names
[('number_customer_service_calls > 2.00', 0.15255665525554568),
 ('total_day_minutes > 213.80', 0.11572355524257688),
 ('number_vmail_messages <= 0.00', 0.09656802173637159),
 ('total_night_calls <= 86.00', 0.07347814323553245),
 ('total_day_calls <= 86.00', 0.03143722302975322),
 ('total_eve_minutes <= 166.20', -0.016279347282555784),
 ('88.00 < total_eve_calls <= 101.00', 0.01202796623602075),
 ('4.00 < total_intl_calls <= 5.00', -0.008862308197327355),
 ('72.00 < account_length <= 98.00', 0.008095316213066618),
 ('total_intl_minutes > 12.00', 0.004036225959225672),
```

```
('200.20 < total_night_minutes <= 234.80',
0.0031930707578459207),
('total_intl_charge > 3.24', -0.0025561403383019586),
('total_day_charge > 36.35', -0.0021799602467677667),
('9.01 < total_night_charge <= 10.57', -0.001598247181850764),
('total_eve_charge <= 14.13', -0.001066803177182677),
('area_code_tr > 1.00', 0.0007760299764712853)]
```

In a similar fashion, the graphs can be generated for different data points from the training sample as well as the test sample.

Recipe 2-16. Model Explanations Using ELI5

Problem

You want to get model explanations using the ELI5 library.

Solution

ELI5 provides two functions to show weights and make predictions to generate model explanations.

How It Works

Let's take a look at the following script:

```
eli5.show_weights(log_model,
                  feature_names=list(xtrain.columns))
```

y=1 top features

Weight?	Feature
+0.449	number_customer_service_calls
+0.010	total_day_minutes
+0.009	total_intl_minutes
+0.002	total_intl_charge
+0.002	total_eve_minutes
+0.001	total_day_charge
+0.000	total_eve_charge
-0.000	total_night_charge
-0.001	total_night_minutes
-0.002	account_length
-0.006	area_code_tr
-0.008	total_day_calls
-0.017	total_eve_calls
-0.017	total_night_calls
-0.034	<BIAS>
-0.037	number_vmail_messages
-0.087	total_intl_calls

```
eli5.explain_weights(log_model, feature_names=list(xtrain.
columns))
```

y=1 top features

Weight?	Feature
+0.449	number_customer_service_calls
+0.010	total_day_minutes
+0.009	total_intl_minutes
+0.002	total_intl_charge
+0.002	total_eve_minutes
+0.001	total_day_charge
+0.000	total_eve_charge
-0.000	total_night_charge
-0.001	total_night_minutes
-0.002	account_length
-0.006	area_code_tr
-0.008	total_day_calls
-0.017	total_eve_calls
-0.017	total_night_calls
-0.034	<BIAS>
-0.037	number_vmail_messages
-0.087	total_intl_calls

```
eli5.explain_prediction(log_model,xtrain.iloc[60])
```

y=0 (probability **0.788**, score **-1.310**) top features

Contribution?	Feature
+2.458	total_night_calls
+1.289	total_eve_calls
+0.698	total_day_calls
+0.304	account_length
+0.174	total_intl_calls
+0.127	total_night_minutes
+0.034	<BIAS>
+0.006	area_code_tr
+0.002	total_night_charge
-0.004	total_intl_charge
-0.005	total_eve_charge
-0.057	total_intl_minutes
-0.064	total_day_charge
-0.304	total_eve_minutes
-0.449	number_customer_service_calls
-2.899	total_day_minutes

```
from eli5.sklearn import PermutationImportance
perm = PermutationImportance(log_model)
perm.fit(xtest, ytest)
eli5.show_weights(perm,feature_names=list(xtrain.columns))
```

Weight	Feature
0.0066 ± 0.0139	number_customer_service_calls
0.0066 ± 0.0024	number_vmail_messages
0.0030 ± 0.0085	total_eve_calls
0.0030 ± 0.0085	total_day_minutes
0.0006 ± 0.0088	total_day_calls
0 ± 0.0000	area_code_tr
0 ± 0.0000	total_intl_charge
0 ± 0.0000	total_night_charge
0 ± 0.0000	total_eve_charge
-0.0012 ± 0.0048	total_intl_calls
-0.0012 ± 0.0029	total_intl_minutes
-0.0024 ± 0.0096	account_length
-0.0024 ± 0.0024	total_day_charge
-0.0036 ± 0.0045	total_night_minutes
-0.0042 ± 0.0061	total_eve_minutes
-0.0048 ± 0.0072	total_night_calls

Conclusion

In this chapter, we covered how to interpret linear supervised models
such as regression and classification. The linear models are simpler to
interpret at a global level, meaning at a feature importance level, but hard
to explain at a local interpretation level. In this chapter, we looked at local
interpretation for samples using the SHAP, ELI5, and LIME libraries.

In the next chapter, we will cover the local and global interpretations for nonlinear models. The nonlinear models cover nonlinearity existing in data and thereby can be complex to interpret. Hence, we need a set of frameworks to explain the nonlinearity in a model.

References

1. Dua, D. and Graff, C. (2019). UCI Machine Learning Repository [http://archive.ics.uci.edu/ml]. Irvine, CA: University of California, School of Information and Computer Science.

## CHAPTER 3

Explainability for Nonlinear Supervised Models

In this chapter, we are going to use explainable libraries to explain a regression model and a classification model, while training a nonlinear model. A nonlinear model is something where either the input variables are transformed using nonlinear transformations or the function to model the input and output is nonlinear.

In the pursuit of achieving higher accuracy, input features are modified either by including polynomial features or by including interaction features, such as additive features and multiplicative features. The benefit of adding nonlinear features is to capture more complexity in the data and catch more complex patterns existing in the data. If we are going to use nonlinear features, the explainability can be followed as per the recipes provided in Chapter 2. If we have a few features, we can create handcrafted

P. Mishra, *Explainable AI Recipes*, https://doi.org/10.1007/978-1-4842-9029-3_3

polynomial features; however, if we have many features, creating all combinations of nonlinear features is not only difficult but also very complex to interpret. Hence, selecting a nonlinear function or a learning algorithm makes life easier. So, we are going to use the ID3 algorithm that powers the decision tree to capture nonlinearity existing in data.

The goal of this chapter is to introduce various explainability libraries for decision tree models such as feature importance, partial dependency plot, and local interpretation.

Recipe 3-1. SHAP Values for Tree Models on All Numerical Input Variables

Problem

You want to explain a decision tree–based regression model built on all numeric features.

Solution

The decision tree–based regression model on all numeric features is trained, and then the trained model will be passed through SHAP to generate global explanations and local explanations.

How It Works

Let's take a look at the following example. The Shapely value can be called the SHAP value. It is used to explain the model and is used for the impartial distribution of predictions from a cooperative game theory to attribute a feature to the model's predictions. Model input features are considered as players in the game. The model function is considered as the rules of the game. The Shapely value of a feature is computed based on the following steps:

1. SHAP requires model retraining on all feature subsets; hence, usually it takes time if the explanation has to be generated for larger datasets.

2. Identify a feature set from a list of features (let's say there are 15 features; we can select a subset with 5 features).

3. For any particular feature, two models using the subset of features will be created, one with the feature and another without the feature.

4. The prediction differences will be computed.

5. The differences in prediction are computed for all possible subsets of features.

6. The weighted average value of all possible differences is used to populate the feature importance.

If the weight of the feature is 0.000, then we can conclude that the feature is not important and has not joined the model. If it is not equal to 0.000, then we can conclude that the feature has a role to play in the prediction process.

We are going to use a dataset from the UCI machine learning repository. The URL to access the dataset is as follows:

```
https://archive.ics.uci.edu/ml/datasets/Appliances+energy+
prediction
```

The objective is to predict the appliances' energy use in Wh, using the features from sensors. There are 27 features in the dataset, and here we are trying to understand what features are important in predicting the energy usage. See Table 3-1.

Table 3-1. *Feature Description from the Energy Prediction Dataset*

Feature Name	Description	Unit
Appliances	Energy use	In Wh
Lights	Energy use of light fixtures in the house	In Wh
T1	Temperature in kitchen area	In Celsius
RH_1	Humidity in kitchen area	In %
T2	Temperature in living room area	In Celsius
RH_2	Humidity in living room area	In %
T3	Temperature in laundry room area	
RH_3	Humidity in laundry room area	In %
T4	Temperature in office room	In Celsius
RH_4	Humidity in office room	In %
T5	Temperature in bathroom	In Celsius
RH_5	Humidity in bathroom	In %
T6	Temperature outside the building (north side)	In Celsius
RH_6	Humidity outside the building (north side)	In %
T7	Temperature in ironing room	In Celsius
RH_7	Humidity in ironing room	In %

(continued)

Table 3-1. (*continued*)

Feature Name	Description	Unit
T8	Temperature in teenager room 2	In Celsius
RH_8	Humidity in teenager room 2	In %
T9	Temperature in parents room	In Celsius
RH_9	Humidity in parents room	In %
To	Temperature outside (from the Chievres weather station)	In Celsius
Pressure (from Chievres weather station)		In mm Hg
aRH_out	Humidity outside (from the Chievres weather station)	In %
Wind speed (from Chievres weather station)		In m/s
Visibility (from Chievres weather station)		In km
Tdewpoint (from Chievres weather station)		Â°C
rv1	Random variable 1	Nondimensional
rv2	Random variable 2	Nondimensional

```
pip install shap

import pandas as pd
df_lin_reg = pd.read_csv('https://archive.ics.uci.edu/ml/
machine-learning-databases/00374/energydata_complete.csv')
del df_lin_reg['date']
df_lin_reg.info()
df_lin_reg.columns
```

```
Index(['Appliances', 'lights', 'T1', 'RH_1', 'T2', 'RH_2',
'T3', 'RH_3', 'T4', 'RH_4', 'T5', 'RH_5', 'T6', 'RH_6', 'T7',
'RH_7', 'T8', 'RH_8', 'T9', 'RH_9', 'T_out', 'Press_mm_hg',
'RH_out', 'Windspeed', 'Visibility', 'Tdewpoint', 'rv1',
'rv2'], dtype='object')
```

```
#y is the dependent variable, that we need to predict
y = df_lin_reg.pop('Appliances')
# X is the set of input features
X = df_lin_reg
```

```
import pandas as pd
import shap
import sklearn
from sklearn import tree, metrics, model_selection,
preprocessing
from IPython.display import Image, display
from sklearn.metrics import confusion_matrix,
classification_report
```

```
# a simple non linear model initialized
model = tree. DecisionTreeRegressor() # plain tree model
```

```
# nonlinear regression model trained
model.fit(X, y)
```

```
tree.plot_tree(model)
```

This produces a complex and messy graph that is difficult to interpret.
See Figure 3-1.

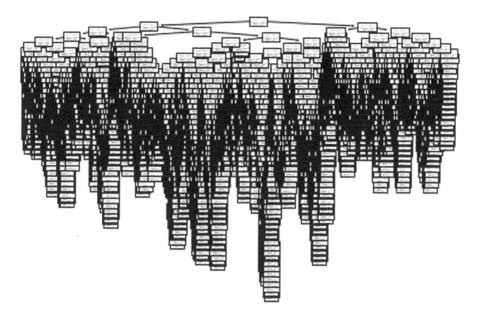

Figure 3-1. *Decision tree model representation*

To explain the decision tree in simple format, the following code can be used:

```
from sklearn.tree import export_text
r = export_text(model,feature_names=list(X.columns))
print(r)
|--- lights <= 5.00
|    |--- RH_out <= 70.92
|    |    |--- T3 <= 26.94
|    |    |    |--- T3 <= 23.25
|    |    |    |    |--- RH_7 <= 27.48
|    |    |    |    |    |--- T5 <= 17.50
|    |    |    |    |    |    |--- RH_5 <= 48.86
|    |    |    |    |    |    |    |--- RH_6 <= 23.91
|    |    |    |    |    |    |    |    |--- RH_1 <= 34.60
|    |    |    |    |    |    |    |    |    |--- value: [610.00]
```

```
|   |   |   |   |   |   |   |   |   |--- RH_1 >  34.60
|   |   |   |   |   |   |   |   |   |--- value: [580.00]
|   |   |   |   |   |   |   |   |--- RH_6 >  23.91
|   |   |   |   |   |   |   |   |--- T3 <= 21.81
..................
```

```
list(zip(model.feature_importances_,X.columns))
```

```
[(0.04755691132990445, 'lights'), (0.02729240744739512,
'T1'), (0.050990867453263464, 'RH_1'), (0.029613682425136578,
'T2'), (0.05287817171439917, 'RH_2'), (0.03809698118314153,
'T3'), (0.04702017020903361, 'RH_3'), (0.03833652568783967,
'T4'), (0.029168659250593493, 'RH_4'), (0.023818050212012467,
'T5'), (0.053380938919333785, 'RH_5'), (0.03242898742121811,
'T6'), (0.036442867206438946, 'RH_6'), (0.03272087870063947,
'T7'), (0.0459966882745736, 'RH_7'), (0.03786926541394416,
'T8'), (0.05569343410157808, 'RH_8'), (0.03888560547088362,
'T9'), (0.03205551180175258, 'RH_9'), (0.018209440939872642,
'T_out'), (0.04401669364414831, 'Press_mm_hg'),
(0.06483375260268251, 'RH_out'), (0.0343793163965324,
'Windspeed'), (0.022764397449413956, 'Visibility'),
(0.02962771107600761, 'Tdewpoint'), (0.023354544387479956,
'rv1'), (0.012567539280780866, 'rv2')]
```

```
# compute the SHAP values for the nonlinear model
explainer = shap.TreeExplainer(model)

# SHAP value calculation
shap_values = explainer.shap_values(X)
```

Recipe 3-2. Partial Dependency Plot for Tree Regression Model

Problem

You want to get a partial dependency plot from a decision tree regression model.

Solution

The solution to this problem is to use a partial dependency plot from the model using a tree explainer. The correlation between the feature and it's SHAP values graphically displayed in Figure 3-2.

How It Works

Let's take a look at the following example:

```
shap.partial_dependence_plot(
    "lights", model.predict, X, ice=False,
    model_expected_value=True, feature_expected_value=True
)
```

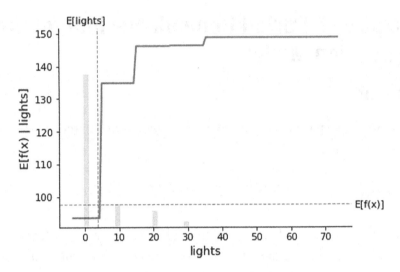

Figure 3-2. *Correlation between feature light and predicted output of the model*

The correlation between the feature lights and the predicted value of the model energy usage is shown, and the steps show a nonlinear pattern.

The partial dependency plot is a way to explain the individual predictions and generate local interpretations for the sample selected from the dataset.

Recipe 3-3. SHAP Feature Importance for Regression Models with All Numerical Input Variables

Problem

You want to calculate the feature importance using the SHAP values from a decision tree–based model.

Solution

The solution to this problem is to use SHAP absolute values from the model.

How It Works

Let's take a look at the following example (see Figure 3-3):

```
import shap
# compute the SHAP values for the linear model
explainer = shap.TreeExplainer(model)

# SHAP value calculation
shap_values = explainer.shap_values(X)

# explain all the predictions in the dataset
shap.summary_plot(shap_values, X)
```

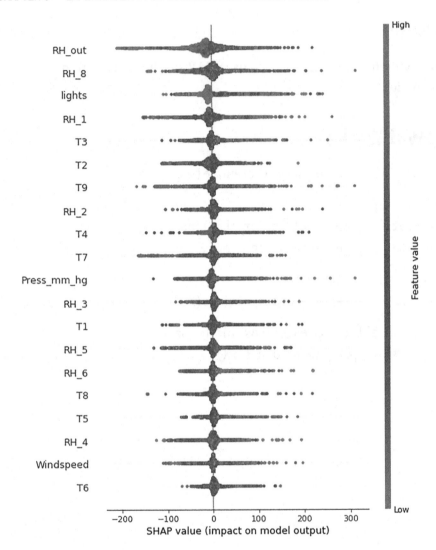

Figure 3-3. *SHAP value-based feature importance plot taken from summary plot*

The decision tree regressor-based model provides the summary plot that contains the SHAP value impact on the model output. if we need to explain the global importance of the features using the SHAP values, which shows not for any individual data point but for all data points what features are important, we can use the summary plot.

Recipe 3-4. SHAP Values for Tree Regression Models with All Mixed Input Variables

Problem

You want to get SHAP values when you have mixed input features such as numerical and categorical.

Solution

Mixed input variables that have numeric features as well as categorical or binary features can be modeled together. As the number of features increases, the time to compute all the permutations will also increase.

How It Works

Let's take a look at the following example. We are going to use a public automobile data dataset with some modifications. The objective is to predict the price of a vehicle given the features such as make, location, age, etc. It is a regression problem that we are going to solve using a mix of numeric and categorical features.

```
df = pd.read_csv('https://raw.githubusercontent.com/
pradmishra1/PublicDatasets/main/automobile.csv')
df.head(3)
df.columns
Index(['Price', 'Make', 'Location', 'Age', 'Odometer',
'FuelType', 'Transmission', 'OwnerType', 'Mileage', 'EngineCC',
'PowerBhp'], dtype='object')
```

We cannot use the string-based features or categorical features in the model directly as matrix multiplication is not possible on string features; hence, the string-based features need to be transformed into dummy variables or binary features with 0 and 1 flags. We are skipping the transformation step here as many data scientists already know how to do data transformation. We are importing another transformed dataset directly.

```
df_t = pd.read_csv('https://raw.githubusercontent.com/
pradmishra1/PublicDatasets/main/Automobile_transformed.csv')
del df_t['Unnamed: 0']
df_t.head(3)
df_t.columns
Index(['Price', 'Age', 'Odometer', 'mileage', 'engineCC',
'powerBhp', 'Location_Bangalore', 'Location_Chennai',
'Location_Coimbatore', 'Location_Delhi', 'Location_Hyderabad',
'Location_Jaipur', 'Location_Kochi', 'Location_Kolkata',
'Location_Mumbai', 'Location_Pune', 'FuelType_Diesel',
'FuelType_Electric', 'FuelType_LPG', 'FuelType_Petrol',
'Transmission_Manual', 'OwnerType_Fourth +ACY- Above',
'OwnerType_Second', 'OwnerType_Third'], dtype='object')

#y is the dependent variable, that we need to predict
y = df_t.pop('Price')
# X is the set of input features
X = df_t

import pandas as pd
import shap
import sklearn

# a simple non linear model initialized
model = sklearn.tree.DecisionTreeRegressor()

# decision tree regression model trained
model.fit(X, y)
```

To compute the SHAP values, we can use the explainer function using the training dataset X and model predict function. The SHAP value calculation happens using a permutation approach that takes 5 minutes.

```
# compute the SHAP values for the linear model
explainer = shap.Explainer(model)

# SHAP value calculation
shap_values = explainer.shap_values(X)
```

Recipe 3-5. SHAP Partial Dependency Plot for Regression Models with Mixed Input
Problem

You want to plot a partial dependency plot and interpret the graph for numeric and categorical dummy variables.

Solution

A partial dependency plot shows the correlation between the feature and the predicted output of the target variables. There are two ways we can showcase the results, one with a feature and expected value of the prediction function and another by superimposing a data point on the partial dependency plot. The nonlinear relationship is shown in Figure 3-4 which is different from a straight line that we have seen in Chapter 2, here it shows a zigzag pattern.

How It Works

Let's take a look at the following example:

```
shap.partial_dependence_plot(
    "powerBhp", model.predict, X, ice=False,
    model_expected_value=True, feature_expected_value=True
)
```

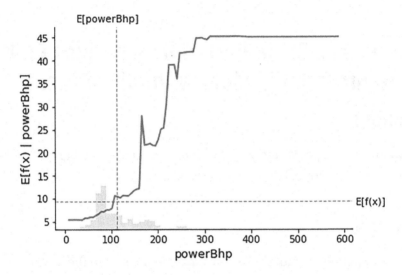

Figure 3-4. *Nonlinear relationship between the powerBhp and the predicted output from the model*

The nonlinear blue line shows the positive correlation between the price and powerBhp. The powerBhp is a strong feature. The higher the bhp, the higher the price of the car. This is a continuous or numeric feature; let's look at the binary or dummy features. There are two dummy features for if the car registered in a Bangalore location or a Kolkata location. Figure 3-5 shows the nonlinear relationship between a dummy variable and it's SHAP value.

```
shap.partial_dependence_plot(
    "Location_Bangalore", model.predict, X, ice=False,
    model_expected_value=True, feature_expected_value=True
)
```

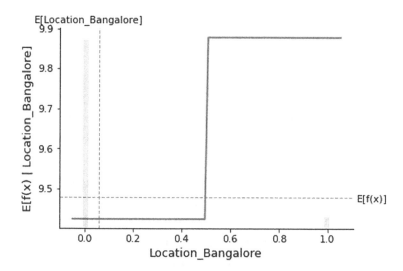

Figure 3-5. *Dummy variable Bangalore location versus SHAP value*

If the location of the car is Bangalore, then the price will be higher, and vice versa.

```
shap.partial_dependence_plot(
    "Location_Kolkata", model.predict, X, ice=False,
    model_expected_value=True, feature_expected_value=True
)
```

The Figure 3-6 shows the relationship like Figure 3-5 but for a different location.

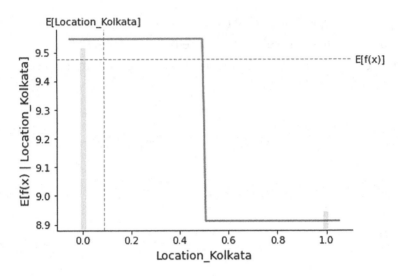

Figure 3-6. *Dummy variable Location_Kolkata versus SHAP value*

If the location is Kolkata, then the price is expected to be lower. The reason for the difference between the two locations is the data that is being used to train the model. The previous three figures show the global importance of a feature versus the prediction function. As an example, only two features are taken into consideration. We can use all features one by one and display many graphs to understand the predictions more.

Recipe 3-6. SHAP Feature Importance for Tree Regression Models with All Mixed Input Variables

Problem

You want to get the global feature importance from SHAP values using mixed input feature data.

Solution

The solution to this problem is to use absolute values and sort them in descending order. The global feature importance for all the features are displayed in Figure 3-7 below.

How It Works

Let's take a look at the following example:

```
list(zip(model.feature_importances_,X.columns))
[(0.169576524767871, 'Age'), (0.046585658464360816,
'Odometer'), (0.04576869739225194, 'mileage'),
(0.059163321062728785, 'engineCC'), (0.6384264191473127,
'powerBhp'), (0.0025223143133269304, 'Location_
Bangalore'), (0.0008970034245261699, 'Location_
Chennai'), (0.003791617161795056, 'Location_
Coimbatore'), (0.0010761093313731759, 'Location_Delhi'),
(0.011285026407948304, 'Location_Hyderabad'),
(0.00020112882138512196, 'Location_Jaipur'),
(0.00086161987910522111, 'Location_Kochi'),
(0.0008846931798977568, 'Location_Kolkata'),
(0.0021470912577561748, 'Location_Mumbai'),
(0.0007076796376248901, 'Location_Pune'),
(0.0013274593267184971, 'FuelType_Diesel'), (0.0,
'FuelType_Electric'), (3.4571613363343374e-07,
'FuelType_LPG'), (0.00242358883910862, 'FuelType_
Petrol'), (0.010550931985109665, 'Transmission_Manual'),
(8.131243463060016e-07, 'OwnerType_Fourth +ACY-
Above'), (0.0016721486214358624, 'OwnerType_Second'),
(0.0003110381011919031, 'OwnerType_Third')]

# explain all the predictions in the dataset
shap.summary_plot(shap_values, X)
```

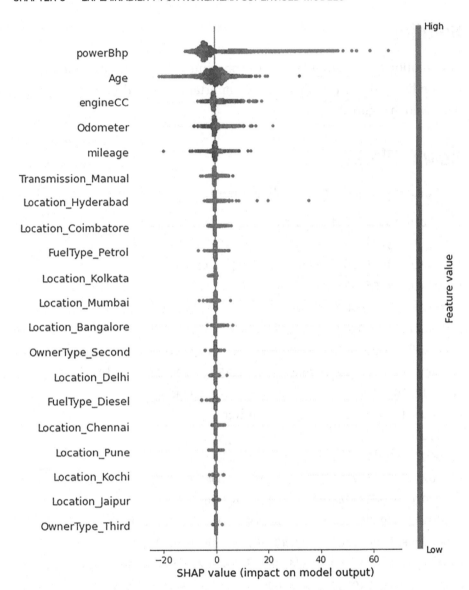

Figure 3-7. *Explaining all predictions with feature importance*

At a high level for the tree-based nonlinear model that is used to predict the price of the automobiles, the previous features are important. The most important are the powerBhp, age of the car, petrol type, manual transmission type, etc. The previous tabular output shows the global feature importance.

Recipe 3-7. LIME Explainer for Tabular Data

Problem

You want to generate the explainability at a local level in a focused manner rather than at a global level.

Solution

The solution to this problem is to use the LIME library. LIME is a model-agnostic technique; it retrains the ML model while running the explainer. LIME localizes a problem and explains the model at a local level.

How It Works

Let's take a look at the following example. LIME requires a numpy array as an input to the tabular explainer; hence, the Pandas dataframe needs to be transformed into an array.

```
!pip install lime
Looking in indexes: https://pypi.org/simple, https://us-python.
pkg.dev/colab-wheels/public/simple/
Collecting lime
  Downloading lime-0.2.0.1.tar.gz (275 kB)
     |███████████████████████████████| 275 kB 3.9 MB/s
Requirement already satisfied: matplotlib in /usr/local/lib/
python3.7/dist-packages (from lime) (3.2.2)
Requirement already satisfied: numpy in /usr/local/lib/
python3.7/dist-packages (from lime) (1.21.6)
Requirement already satisfied: scipy in /usr/local/lib/
python3.7/dist-packages (from lime) (1.7.3)
```

```
Require
. . . . . . . . . . . . . .
import lime
import lime.lime_tabular

explainer = lime.lime_tabular.LimeTabularExplainer(np.array(X),
                                          mode=
                                          'regression',
                                          feature_names=
                                          X.columns,
                                          class_
                                          names=['price'],
                                          verbose=True)
```

We are using the energy prediction data from this chapter only.

```
explainer.feature_selection

# asking for explanation for LIME model
i = 60
exp = explainer.explain_instance(np.array(X)[i],
                          model.predict,
                          num_features=14
                          )
```

We do not have to retrain the decision tree model. We can pass the model object obtained from training a decision tree model and reuse it with the LIME explainer. Figure 3-8 shows the location explanation for the 60th record from the training dataset.

```
model.predict(X)[60]

X[60:61]
Intercept -6.9881095432071465
Prediction_local [33.29071077]
Right: 16.5
```

```
exp.show_in_notebook(show_table=True)
```

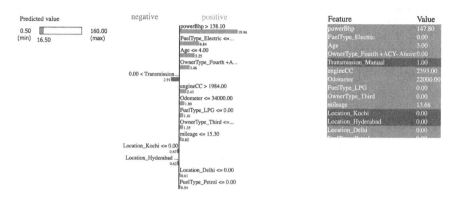

Figure 3-8. *Local explanation for the 60ᵗʰ record from the dataset*

```
exp.as_list()
[('powerBhp > 138.10', 19.961371959849174), ('FuelType_
Electric <= 0.00', 6.836722688525879), ('Age <= 4.00',
5.249921722968705), ('OwnerType_Fourth +ACY- Above <=
0.00', 3.4582886724264483), ('0.00 < Transmission_
Manual <= 1.00', -2.9145492368305157), ('engineCC >
1984.00', 2.432167151933345), ('Odometer <= 34000.00',
1.8038639987179637), ('FuelType_LPG <= 0.00',
1.4135278408858953), ('OwnerType_Third <= 0.00',
1.3547839120439655), ('mileage <= 15.30', 0.8239170366232045),
('Location_Kochi <= 0.00', -0.6740434016444569), ('Location_
Hyderabad <= 0.00', -0.6190270673151664), ('Location_Delhi
<= 0.00', 0.6091569397933114), ('FuelType_Petrol <= 0.00',
0.5427180987401807)]
```

Recipe 3-8. ELI5 Explainer for Tabular Data

Problem

You want to use the ELI5 library to generate explanations of a linear regression model.

Solution

ELI5 is a Python package that helps to debug a machine learning model and explain the predictions. It provides support for all machine learning models supported by the scikit-learn library.

How It Works

Let's take a look at the following example:

```
pip install eli5
import eli5
eli5.show_weights(model,
                feature_names=list(X.columns))
```

Weight	Feature
0.6384	powerBhp
0.1696	Age
0.0592	engineCC
0.0466	Odometer
0.0458	Mileage
0.0113	Location_Hyderabad
0.0106	Transmission_Manual

(continued)

Weight	Feature
0.0038	Location_Coimbatore
0.0025	Location_Bangalore
0.0022	FuelType_Petrol
0.0021	Location_Mumbai
0.0017	OwnerType_Second
0.0013	FuelType_Diesel
0.0011	Location_Delhi
0.0009	Location_Chennai
0.0009	Location_Kolkata
0.0009	Location_Kochi
0.0007	Location_Pune
0.0003	OwnerType_Third
0.0002	Location_Jaipu

```
eli5.explain_weights(model, feature_names=list(X.columns))
```

Weight	Feature
0.6384	powerBhp
0.1696	Age
0.0592	engineCC
0.0466	Odometer
0.0458	Mileage
0.0113	Location_Hyderabad
0.0106	Transmission_Manual

(continued)

97

Weight	Feature
0.0038	Location_Coimbatore
0.0025	Location_Bangalore
0.0022	FuelType_Petrol
0.0021	Location_Mumbai
0.0017	OwnerType_Second
0.0013	FuelType_Diesel
0.0011	Location_Delhi
0.0009	Location_Chennai
0.0009	Location_Kolkata
0.0009	Location_Kochi
0.0007	Location_Pune
0.0003	OwnerType_Third
0.0002	Location_Jaipur

eli5.explain_prediction(model,X.iloc[60])

y (score **16.500**) top features

Contribution?	Feature
+9.479	<BIAS>
+4.710	engineCC
+4.190	Age
+1.467	mileage
+0.713	FuelType_Petrol
+0.667	powerBhp

(*continued*)

Contribution?	Feature
+0.071	Odometer
-1.313	Location_Mumbai
-3.485	Transmission_Manual

```
from eli5.sklearn import PermutationImportance

# a simple linear model initialized
model = sklearn.tree.DecisionTreeRegressor()

# linear regression model trained
model.fit(X, y)

perm = PermutationImportance(model)
perm.fit(X, y)
eli5.show_weights(perm,feature_names=list(X.columns))
```

Weight	Feature
1.3784 ± 0.0884	powerBhp
0.4245 ± 0.0049	Age
0.2587 ± 0.0120	engineCC
0.1968 ± 0.0333	Odometer
0.1557 ± 0.0103	mileage
0.0709 ± 0.0425	Location_Hyderabad
0.0550 ± 0.0076	Transmission_Manual
0.0120 ± 0.0037	FuelType_Petrol
0.0095 ± 0.0011	Location_Coimbatore
0.0086 ± 0.0015	FuelType_Diesel

(continued)

Weight	Feature
0.0071 ± 0.0013	Location_Mumbai
0.0058 ± 0.0016	Location_Bangalore
0.0054 ± 0.0011	OwnerType_Second
0.0030 ± 0.0005	Location_Kolkata
0.0030 ± 0.0012	Location_Kochi
0.0030 ± 0.0003	Location_Delhi
0.0027 ± 0.0011	Location_Chennai
0.0017 ± 0.0003	Location_Pune
0.0004 ± 0.0001	Location_Jaipur
0.0002 ± 0.0001	OwnerType_Thir

The results table has a BIAS value as a feature. This can be interpreted as an intercept term for a linear regression model. Other features are listed based on the descending order of importance based on their weight. The show weights function provides a global interpretation of the model, and the show prediction function provides a local interpretation by taking into account a record from the training set.

Recipe 3-9. How the Permutation Model in ELI5 Works

Problem

You want to make sense of the ELI5 permutation library.

Solution

The solution to this problem is to use a dataset and a trained model.

How It Works

The permutation model in the ELI5 library works only for global interpretation. First it takes a base line linear regression model from the training dataset and computes the error of the model. Then it shuffles the values of a feature, retrains the model, and computes the error. It compares the decrease in error after shuffling and before shuffling. A feature can be considered as important if post shuffling the error delta is high and unimportant if the error delta is low, and vice versa. The result displays the average importance of features and the standard deviation of features with multiple shuffle steps.

Recipe 3-10. Global Explanation for Decision Tree Models

Problem

You want to explain the predictions generated from a decision tree classifier.

Solution

The decision tree model can be used as we model the probabilities from either a binary classification or a multinomial classification variable. In this particular recipe, we are using a churn classification dataset that has two outcomes: whether the customer is likely to churn or not.

How It Works

Let's take a look at the following example. The key is to get the SHAP values, which will return base values, SHAP values, and data. Using the SHAP values, we can create various explanations using graphs and figures. The SHAP values are always at a global level.

```python
import pandas as pd
import numpy as np
import matplotlib.pyplot as plt
%matplotlib inline
from sklearn import tree, metrics, model_selection,
preprocessing
from sklearn.metrics import confusion_matrix,
classification_report

df_train = pd.read_csv('https://raw.githubusercontent.com/
pradmishra1/PublicDatasets/main/ChurnData_test.csv')
from sklearn.preprocessing import LabelEncoder

tras = LabelEncoder()
df_train['area_code_tr'] = tras.fit_transform(df_
train['area_code'])
df_train.columns
del df_train['area_code']
df_train.columns
df_train['target_churn_dum'] = pd.get_dummies(df_train.
churn,prefix='churn',drop_first=True)
df_train.columns
del df_train['international_plan']
del df_train['voice_mail_plan']
del df_train['churn']
df_train.info()
```

```python
del df_train['Unnamed: 0']
df_train.columns
from sklearn.model_selection import train_test_split

df_train.columns

X = df_train[['account_length', 'number_vmail_messages',
'total_day_minutes',
        'total_day_calls', 'total_day_charge', 'total_eve_
        minutes',
        'total_eve_calls', 'total_eve_charge', 'total_night_
        minutes',
        'total_night_calls', 'total_night_charge', 'total_intl_
        minutes',
        'total_intl_calls', 'total_intl_charge',
        'number_customer_service_calls', 'area_code_tr']]
Y = df_train['target_churn_dum']

xtrain,xtest,ytrain,ytest=train_test_split(X,Y,test_
size=0.20,stratify=Y)
tree_model = tree.DecisionTreeClassifier()

tree_model.fit(xtrain,ytrain)

print("training accuracy:", tree_model.score(xtrain,ytrain))
#training accuracy

print("test accuracy:",tree_model.score(xtest,ytest)) # test
accuracy
training accuracy: 1.0
test accuracy: 0.8562874251497006

# Provide Probability as Output
def model_churn_proba(x):
    return tree_model.predict_proba(x)[:,1]
```

```
# Provide Log Odds as Output
def model_churn_log_odds(x):
    p = tree_model.predict_log_proba(x)
    return p[:,1] - p[:,0]

# compute the SHAP values for the linear model
background_churn = shap.maskers.Independent(X, max_samples=500)
explainer = shap.Explainer(tree_model, background_
churn,feature_names=list(X.columns))
shap_values_churn = explainer(X)
```

Recipe 3-11. Partial Dependency Plot for a Nonlinear Classifier

Problem

You want to show feature associations with the class probabilities using a nonlinear classifier.

Solution

The class probabilities in this example are related to predicting the probability of churn. The SHAP value for a feature can be plotted against the feature value to show a scatter chart that displays the correlation positive or negative and strength of associations. The relationship visually shown in Figure 3-9 below.

How It Works

Let's take a look at the following example:

```
# make a standard partial dependence plot
sample_ind = 25
```

```
fig,ax = shap.partial_dependence_plot(
    "total_day_minutes", model_churn_proba, X, model_expected_
    value=True,
    feature_expected_value=True, show=False, ice=False
)
```

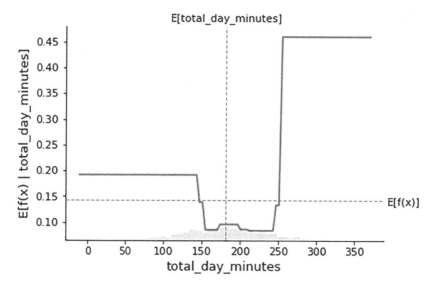

Figure 3-9. *Account length and SHAP value of account length*

```
# make a standard partial dependence plot
sample_ind = 25
fig,ax = shap.partial_dependence_plot(
    "number_vmail_messages", model_churn_proba, X, model_
    expected_value=True,
    feature_expected_value=True, show=False,ice=False)
```

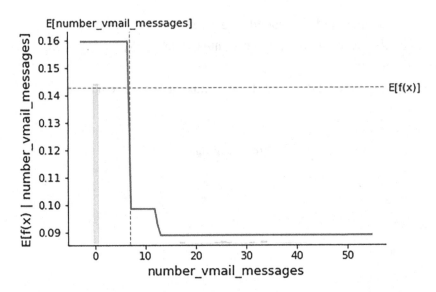

Figure 3-10. *Number of voicemail messages and the SHAP value*

Figure 3-11 compares this with the linear classifier from Chapter 2.

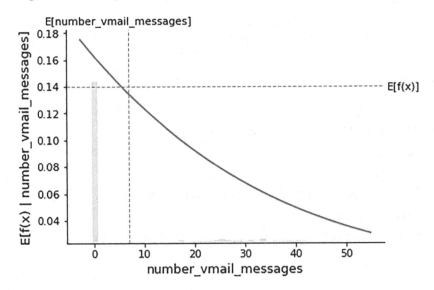

Figure 3-11. *Linear classifier from Chapter 2*

The difference between the two plots is clear. A linear classifier is a downward sloping line, whereas a decision tree classifier has a nonlinear stepwise line.

Recipe 3-12. Global Feature Importance from the Nonlinear Classifier

Problem

You want to get the global feature importance for the decision tree classification model.

Solution

The solution to this problem is to use explainer log odds.

How It Works

Let's take a look at the following example:

```
# compute the SHAP values for the linear model
explainer_log_odds = shap.Explainer(tree_model, background_
churn,feature_names=list(X.columns))
shap_values_churn_log_odds = explainer_log_odds(X)
shap_values_churn_log_odds

temp_df = pd.DataFrame()
temp_df['Feature Name'] = pd.Series(X.columns)
temp_df['Importance'] = pd.Series(tree_model.feature_
importances_)
temp_df.sort_values(by='Importance',ascending=False)
```

	Feature Name	Importance
2	total_day_minutes	0.219502
14	number_customer_service_calls	0.120392
4	total_day_charge	0.097044
7	total_eve_charge	0.095221
1	number_vmail_messages	0.062609
10	total_night_charge	0.061233
8	total_night_minutes	0.057162
9	total_night_calls	0.055642
11	total_intl_minutes	0.046794
3	total_day_calls	0.043435
12	total_intl_calls	0.040072
0	account_length	0.032119
6	total_eve_calls	0.029836
13	total_intl_charge	0.020441
5	total_eve_minutes	0.013121
15	area_code_tr	0.005378

Recipe 3-13. Local Explanations Using LIME

Problem

You want to get faster explanations from explainable both global and local libraries.

Solution

The model explanation can be done using SHAP; however, one of the limitations of SHAP is that we cannot use the full data to create global and local explanations. Even if we decide to use the full data, it usually takes more time. Hence, speeding up the process of generating local and global explanations in a scenario when millions of records are being used to train a model LIME is very useful. The local explanations for 1st record is displayed in Figure 3-12 and 20th record is shown in Figure 3-13.

How It Works

Let's take a look at the following example:

```
import lime
import lime.lime_tabular

explainer = lime.lime_tabular.LimeTabularExplainer(np.
array(xtrain),
                     feature_names=list(xtrain.columns),
                     class_names=['target_churn_dum'],
                     verbose=True, mode='classification')
# this record is a no churn scenario
exp = explainer.explain_instance(xtest.iloc[0], tree_model.
predict_proba, num_features=16)
exp.as_list()
Intercept 0.17857751096606778
Prediction_local [0.16068057]
Right: 1.0
X does not have valid feature names, but DecisionTreeClassifier
was fitted with feature names
[('total_day_minutes > 215.90', 0.1362643566581409),
 ('number_vmail_messages <= 0.00', 0.0929673100640601),
 ('3.00 < total_intl_calls <= 4.00', -0.05389996557257846),
```

```
('total_day_calls <= 86.00', -0.051572104790178076),
('99.00 < total_night_calls <= 112.00',
-0.046773114913399146),
('1.00 < number_customer_service_calls <= 2.00',
-0.04441521857295649),
('total_intl_charge <= 2.32', -0.02367171273632465),
('200.40 < total_eve_minutes <= 232.60',
-0.01768355201942605),
('8.95 < total_night_charge <= 10.40', -0.016767719469372562),
('88.00 < total_eve_calls <= 101.00', -0.015113160995228619),
('total_day_charge > 36.70', 0.01338384802674405),
('area_code_tr > 1.00', 0.006774852953278585),
('total_intl_minutes <= 8.60', 0.005598720978761775),
('17.03 < total_eve_charge <= 19.77', -0.0036223084182909603),
('98.00 < account_length <= 126.00', 0.0006345376072269405),
('198.80 < total_night_minutes <= 231.20',
-1.7083964912392244e-06)]
```

```
pd.DataFrame(exp.as_list())
```

	0	1
0	total_day_minutes > 215.90	0.136264
1	number_vmail_messages <= 0.00	0.092967
2	3.00 < total_intl_calls <= 4.00	-0.053900
3	total_day_calls <= 86.00	-0.051572
4	99.00 < total_night_calls <= 112.00	-0.046773
5	1.00 < number_customer_service_calls <= 2.00	-0.044415
6	total_intl_charge <= 2.32	-0.023672

(continued)

0	1	
7	200.40 < total_eve_minutes <= 232.60	-0.017684
8	8.95 < total_night_charge <= 10.40	-0.016768
9	88.00 < total_eve_calls <= 101.00	-0.015113
10	total_day_charge > 36.70	0.013384
11	area_code_tr > 1.00	0.006775
12	total_intl_minutes <= 8.60	0.005599
13	17.03 < total_eve_charge <= 19.77	-0.003622
14	98.00 < account_length <= 126.00	0.000635
15	198.80 < total_night_minutes <= 231.20	-0.000002

```
exp.show_in_notebook(show_table=True)
```

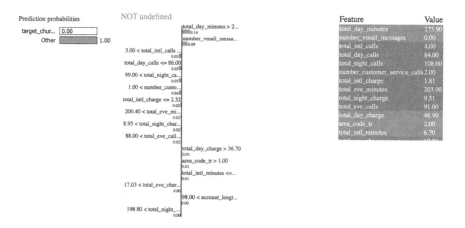

Figure 3-12. *Local explanation for record number 1 from test set*

```
# This is s churn scenario
exp = explainer.explain_instance(xtest.iloc[20], tree_model.
predict_proba, num_features=16)
exp.as_list()
```

```
Intercept 0.10256094438264549
Prediction_local [0.42951224]
Right: 1.0
X does not have valid feature names, but DecisionTreeClassifier
was fitted with feature names
[('number_vmail_messages <= 0.00', 0.1251461520949672),
 ('number_customer_service_calls <= 1.00',
 -0.11471932451025148),
 ('total_day_minutes > 215.90', 0.11335292810078498),
 ('total_intl_calls <= 3.00', 0.0833975606666818),
 ('total_eve_charge > 19.77', 0.07087970621129276),
 ('total_day_charge > 36.70', 0.044322021446899056),
 ('total_night_calls <= 86.00', 0.03835204203269277),
 ('10.40 < total_intl_minutes <= 12.00',
 -0.028762467921123958),
 ('total_eve_calls <= 88.00', 0.027744744266104262),
 ('198.80 < total_night_minutes <= 231.20',
 -0.014434614677050405),
 ('8.95 < total_night_charge <= 10.40', -0.01246344270348464),
 ('86.00 < total_day_calls <= 99.00', 0.012186288614633462),
 ('73.00 < account_length <= 98.00', -0.011046720698750234),
 ('0.00 < area_code_tr <= 1.00', -0.010595644578095056),
 ('2.81 < total_intl_charge <= 3.24', 0.0033945972331523373),
 ('total_eve_minutes > 232.60', 0.0001974706449185791)]

exp.show_in_notebook(show_table=True)
```

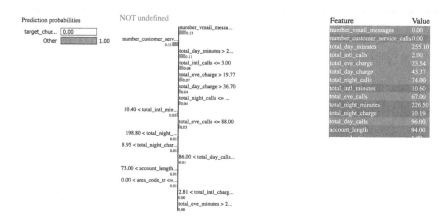

Figure 3-13. *Local explanations from the 20th record from the test set*

In a similar fashion, the graphs can be generated for different records from the training set and test set, which are from the training sample as well as the test sample.

Recipe 3-14. Model Explanations Using ELI5

Problem

You want to get model explanations using the ELI5 library.

Solution

ELI5 provides two functions, show weights and show predictions, to generate model explanations.

113

How It Works

Let's take a look at the following example:

```
Pip install eli5
eli5.show_weights(tree_model,
            feature_names=list(xtrain.columns))
```

Weight	Feature
0.2195	total_day_minutes
0.1204	number_customer_service_calls
0.0970	total_day_charge
0.0952	total_eve_charge
0.0626	number_vmail_messages
0.0612	total_night_charge
0.0572	total_night_minutes
0.0556	total_night_calls
0.0468	total_intl_minutes
0.0434	total_day_calls
0.0401	total_intl_calls
0.0321	account_length
0.0298	total_eve_calls
0.0204	total_intl_charge
0.0131	total_eve_minutes
0.0054	area_code_tr

```
eli5.explain_weights(tree_model, feature_names=list(xtrain.
columns))
```

Weight	Feature
0.2195	total_day_minutes
0.1204	number_customer_service_calls
0.0970	total_day_charge
0.0952	total_eve_charge
0.0626	number_vmail_messages
0.0612	total_night_charge
0.0572	total_night_minutes
0.0556	total_night_calls
0.0468	total_intl_minutes
0.0434	total_day_calls
0.0401	total_intl_calls
0.0321	account_length
0.0298	total_eve_calls
0.0204	total_intl_charge
0.0131	total_eve_minutes
0.0054	area_code_tr

```
eli5.explain_prediction(tree_model,xtrain.iloc[60])
```

y=0 (probability **1.000**) top features

Contribution?	Feature
+0.866	<BIAS>
+0.126	total_eve_charge
+0.118	total_night_charge

(continued)

Contribution?	Feature
+0.076	total_night_calls
+0.038	total_day_minutes
+0.032	number_customer_service_calls
+0.010	total_intl_calls
-0.084	total_eve_calls
-0.088	total_day_calls
-0.093	total_intl_minutes

```
from eli5.sklearn import PermutationImportance
perm = PermutationImportance(tree_model)
perm.fit(xtest, ytest)
eli5.show_weights(perm,feature_names=list(xtrain.columns))
```

Weight	Feature
0.0814 ± 0.0272	total_day_minutes
0.0407 ± 0.0188	number_customer_service_calls
0.0359 ± 0.0085	total_eve_charge
0.0299 ± 0.0147	total_night_minutes
0.0263 ± 0.0198	total_night_charge
0.0210 ± 0.0126	number_vmail_messages
0.0174 ± 0.0088	total_day_charge
0.0042 ± 0.0061	total_intl_charge
0.0036 ± 0.0167	total_intl_minutes
0.0006 ± 0.0024	area_code_tr

(continued)

Weight	Feature
-0.0006 ± 0.0122	total_eve_calls
-0.0012 ± 0.0145	total_eve_minutes
-0.0024 ± 0.0024	account_length
-0.0030 ± 0.0076	total_night_calls
-0.0054 ± 0.0079	total_day_calls
-0.0114 ± 0.0088	total_intl_calls

Conclusion

In this chapter, we covered how to interpret nonlinear supervised models based on decision trees for regression and classification. However, the nonlinear models are simpler to interpret at a global level, meaning at the feature importance level, but hard to explain at the local interpretation level as all the features will not be part of the decision tree construction process. In this chapter, we looked at local interpretation for samples using the SHAP, ELI5, and LIME libraries. In the next chapter, we are going to cover the local and global interpretations for ensemble models. The nonlinear models cover nonlinearity existing in data and therefore can be complex to interpret. However, one of the limitations of a tree-based model is that it only considers a few powerful features to construct the tree and does not give equal importance to all the features. Therefore, the explainability is not complete for local interpretations. This problem can be addressed by ensemble models, which is a combination of many trees working together to make it happen.

CHAPTER 4

Explainability for Ensemble Supervised Models

Ensemble models are considered to be effective when individual models are failing to balance bias and variance for a training dataset. The predictions are aggregated in ensemble models to generate the final models. In the case of supervised regression models, many models are generated, and the averages of all the predictions are taken into consideration to generate the final prediction. Similarly, for supervised classification problems, multiple models are being trained, and each model generates a classification. The final model takes into account the majority voting rule criteria to decide the final prediction. Because of the nature of ensemble models, these are harder to explain to end users. That is why we need frameworks that can explain the ensemble models.

Ensemble means a grouping of the model predictions. There are three types of ensemble models: bagging, boosting, and stacking. *Bagging* means bootstrap aggregation, which means bootstrapping the available features, making a subset selection, generating predictions, continuing the same process a few times, and averaging the predictions to generate the final prediction. Random forest is one of the most important and popular bagging models.

© Pradeepta Mishra 2023
P. Mishra, *Explainable AI Recipes*, https://doi.org/10.1007/978-1-4842-9029-3_4

Boosting is a sequential method of boosting the predictive power of the model. It starts with a base classifier being trained on data to predict and classify the output. In the next step, the correctly predicted cases are separated in an automatic fashion, and the rest of the cases are used for retraining the model. This process will continue until there is a scope to improve and boost the accuracy to a higher level. If it is not possible to boost the accuracy further, then the iteration should stop, and the final accuracy is reported.

Stacking is a process of generating predictions from different sets of models and averaging their predictions.

The goal of this chapter is to introduce various explainability libraries for ensemble models such as feature importance, partial dependency plot, and local interpretation and global interpretation of the models.

Recipe 4-1. Explainable Boosting Machine Interpretation

Problem

You want to explain the explainable boosting machine (EBM) as an ensemble model and interpret the global and local interpretations.

Solution

EBMs are a tree-based, cyclic, gradient descent–based boosting model known as a *generalized additive model* (GAM), which has automatic interaction detection. EBMs are interpretable though they are black box by nature. We need an additional library known as *interpret core*.

How It Works

Let's take a look at the following example. The Shapely value can be called the SHAP value. SHAP value is used to explain the model and is used for the impartial distribution of predictions from a cooperative game theory to attribute a feature to the model's predictions. The model input features are considered as players in the game. The model function is considered as the rules of the game. The Shapely value of a feature is computed based on the following steps:

1. SHAP requires model retraining on all feature subsets; hence, usually it takes time if the explanation has to be generated for larger datasets.

2. Identify a feature set from a list of features (let's say there are 15 features; we can select a subset with 5 features).

3. For any particular feature, two models using the subset of features will be created, one with the feature and another without the feature.

4. The prediction differences will be computed.

5. The differences in prediction are computed for all possible subsets of features.

6. The weighted average value of all possible differences is used to populate the feature importance.

If the weight of the feature is 0.000, then we can conclude that the feature is not important and has not joined the model. If it is not equal to 0.000, then we can conclude that the feature has a role to play in the prediction process.

We are going to use a dataset from the UCI machine learning repository. The URL to access the dataset is as follows:

```
https://archive.ics.uci.edu/ml/datasets/Appliances+energy+
prediction
```

The objective is to predict the appliances' energy use in Wh, using the features from sensors. There are 27 features in the dataset, and here we are trying to understand what features are important in predicting the energy usage. See Table 4-1.

Table 4-1. *Feature Description from the Energy Prediction Dataset*

Feature Name	Description	Unit
Appliances	Energy use	In Wh
Lights	Energy use of light fixtures in the house	In Wh
T1	Temperature in kitchen area	In Celsius
RH_1	Humidity in kitchen area	In %
T2	Temperature in living room area	In Celsius
RH_2	Humidity in living room area	In %
T3	Temperature in laundry room area	
RH_3	Humidity in laundry room area	In %
T4	Temperature in office room	In Celsius
RH_4	Humidity in office room	In %
T5	Temperature in bathroom	In Celsius
RH_5	Humidity in bathroom	In %
T6	Temperature outside the building (north side)	In Celsius

(*continued*)

Table 4-1. (*continued*)

Feature Name	Description	Unit
RH_6	Humidity outside the building (north side)	In %
T7	Temperature in ironing room	In Celsius
RH_7	Humidity in ironing room	In %
T8	Temperature in teenager room 2	In Celsius
RH_8	Humidity in teenager room 2	In %
T9	Temperature in parents room	In Celsius
RH_9	Humidity in parents room	In %
To	Temperature outside (from the Chievres weather station)	In Celsius
Pressure (from Chievres weather station)		In mm Hg
aRH_out	Humidity outside (from the Chievres weather station)	In %
Wind speed (from Chievres weather station)		In m/s
Visibility (from Chievres weather station)		In km
Tdewpoint (from Chievres weather station)		Â°C
rv1	Random variable 1	Nondimensional
rv2	Random variable 2	Nondimensional

```
pip install shap
!pip install interpret-core #this installation is without any
dependency library
Looking in indexes: https://pypi.org/simple, https://us-python.
pkg.dev/colab-wheels/public/simple/
Requirement already satisfied: interpret-core in /usr/local/
lib/python3.7/dist-packages (0.2.7)
```

```
import pandas as pd
df_lin_reg = pd.read_csv('https://archive.ics.uci.edu/ml/
machine-learning-databases/00374/energydata_complete.csv')
del df_lin_reg['date']
df_lin_reg.info()
df_lin_reg.columns
Index(['Appliances', 'lights', 'T1', 'RH_1', 'T2', 'RH_2',
'T3', 'RH_3', 'T4', 'RH_4', 'T5', 'RH_5', 'T6', 'RH_6', 'T7',
'RH_7', 'T8', 'RH_8', 'T9', 'RH_9', 'T_out', 'Press_mm_hg',
'RH_out', 'Windspeed', 'Visibility', 'Tdewpoint', 'rv1',
'rv2'], dtype='object')
```

```
#y is the dependent variable, that we need to predict
y = df_lin_reg.pop('Appliances')
# X is the set of input features
X = df_lin_reg
```

```
# fit a GAM model to the data
import interpret.glassbox
import shap
model_ebm = interpret.glassbox.ExplainableBoostingRegressor()
model_ebm.fit(X, y)
X100 = X[:100]
```

```
# explain the GAM model with SHAP
```

```
explainer_ebm = shap.Explainer(model_ebm.predict, X100)
shap_values_ebm = explainer_ebm(X100)

import numpy as np
pd.DataFrame(np.round(shap_values_ebm.values,2)).head(2)
```

	0	1	2	3	4	5	6	7	8	9	...	17	18	19	20	21	22	23	24	25	26
0	49.18	18.75	-4.06	-5.04	-6.95	3.09	-26.46	-2.34	1.11	-5.25	...	2.6	7.02	-13.1	-1.88	-1.7	22.44	2.01	9.05	2.20	1.81
1	49.18	18.75	-4.73	-5.04	-6.95	3.09	-33.46	-2.34	-5.42	-5.25	...	2.6	7.02	-12.9	-1.88	-1.7	7.94	19.30	9.25	-0.23	-0.04

2 rows × 27 columns

```
pd.DataFrame(np.round(shap_values_ebm.base_values,2)).head(2)
00103.741103.74
```

Recipe 4-2. Partial Dependency Plot for Tree Regression Models

Problem

You want to get a partial dependency plot from a boosting model.

Solution

The solution to this problem is to use a partial dependency plot from the model using SHAP.

How It Works

Let's take a look at the following example (see Figure 4-1):

```
# make a standard partial dependence plot with a single SHAP
value overlaid
sample_ind = 20
```

125

```
fig,ax = shap.partial_dependence_plot(
    "lights", model_ebm.predict, X100, model_expected_
    value=True,
    feature_expected_value=True, show=False, ice=False,
    shap_values=shap_values_ebm[sample_ind:sample_ind+1,:]
)
```

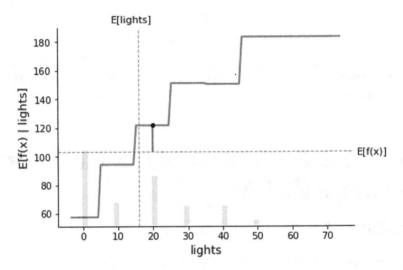

Figure 4-1. *Correlation between feature light and predicted output of the model*

The correlation between the feature lights and the predicted value of the model energy usage is shown, and the steps show a nonlinear pattern. The partial dependency plot is a way to explain the individual predictions and generate local interpretations for the sample selected from the dataset. See Figure 4-2.

```
shap.plots.scatter(shap_values_ebm[:,"lights"])
```

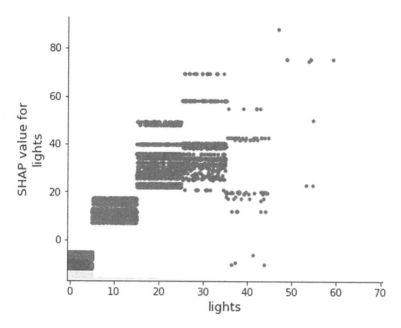

Figure 4-2. *Correlation between the feature lights and the*
SHAP values

```
# the waterfall_plot shows how we get from explainer.expected_
value to model.predict(X)[sample_ind]
shap.plots.waterfall(shap_values_ebm[sample_ind], max_
display=14)
```

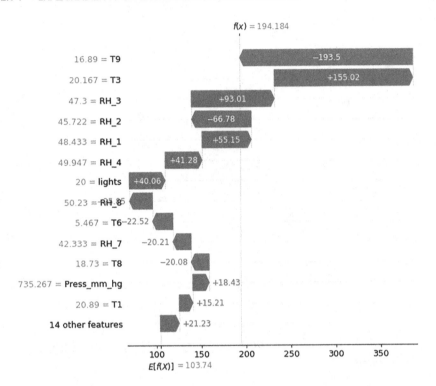

Figure 4-3. *Feature importance for a specific sample record, local interpretation*

```
# the waterfall_plot shows how we get from explainer.expected_
value to model.predict(X)[sample_ind]
shap.plots.beeswarm(shap_values_ebm, max_display=14)
```

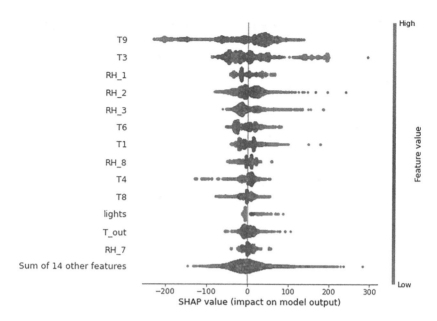

Figure 4-4. *SHAP values' impact on the model output, global exxplanation*

To generate the global explainer, we need to install another visualization library.

```
!pip install dash_cytoscape
from interpret import set_visualize_provider
from interpret.provider import InlineProvider
set_visualize_provider(InlineProvider())
from interpret import show

ebm_global = model_ebm.explain_global()
show(ebm_global)
```

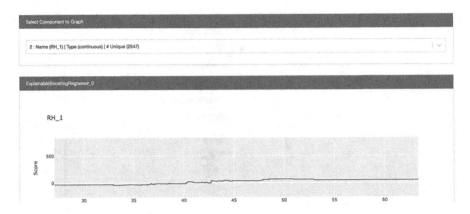

Figure 4-5. *Selecting features from the drop-down to see its contribution*

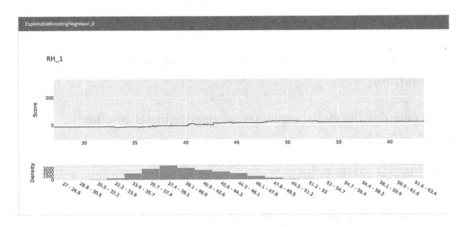

Figure 4-6. *Score of feature RH_1 and its distribution, global interpretation*

```
ebm_local = model_ebm.explain_local(X[:5], y[:5])
show(ebm_local)
ebm_local
```

```
import numpy as np
pd.DataFrame(np.round(shap_values_ebm.values,2)).head(2)
```

```
pd.DataFrame(np.round(shap_values_ebm.base_values,2)).head(2)
```

Recipe 4-3. Explain a Extreme Gradient Boosting Model with All Numerical Input Variables

Problem

You want to explain the extreme gradient boosting–based regressor.

Solution

The XGB regressor can be explained using the SHAP library; we can populate the global and local interpretations.

How It Works

Let's take a look at the following example:

```
# train XGBoost model
import xgboost
model_xgb = xgboost.XGBRegressor(n_estimators=100, max_
depth=2).fit(X, y)

# explain the GAM model with SHAP
explainer_xgb = shap.Explainer(model_xgb, X)
shap_values_xgb = explainer_xgb(X)

# make a standard partial dependence plot with a single SHAP
value overlaid
sample_ind = 18
fig,ax = shap.partial_dependence_plot(
    "lights", model_xgb.predict, X, model_expected_value=True,
    feature_expected_value=True, show=False, ice=False,
    shap_values=shap_values_xgb[sample_ind:sample_ind+1,:]
)
```

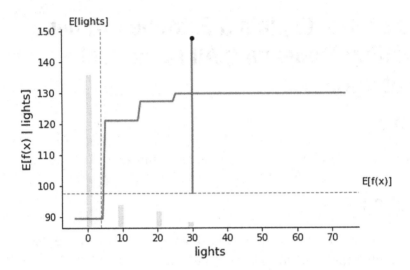

Figure 4-7. *SHAP value–based feature importance plot taken from the summary plot*

The XGB regressor–based model provides the summary plot that contains the SHAP value impact on the model output. If we need to explain the global importance of the features using the SHAP values, which shows what features are important for all data points, we can use the summary plot.

```
shap.plots.scatter(shap_values_xgb[:,"lights"])
```

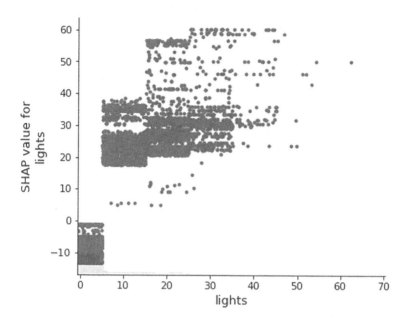

Figure 4-8. *SHAP values of the lights feature plotted against the lights feature*

```
shap.plots.scatter(shap_values_xgb[:,"lights"], color=shap_
values_xgb)
```

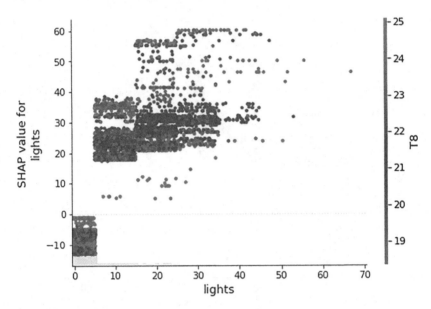

Figure 4-9. *Scatter plot of two features, T8 and lights, against the SHAP values of light*

```
shap.summary_plot(shap_values_xgb, X)
```

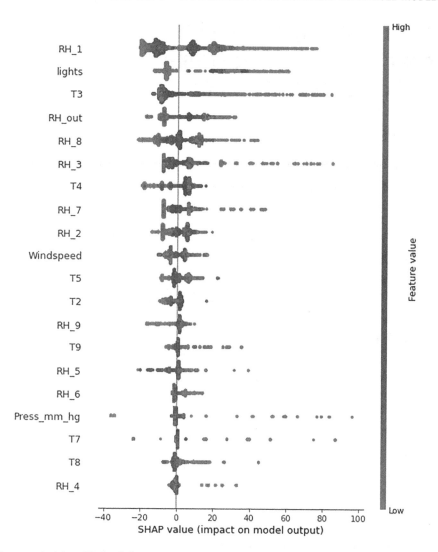

Figure 4-10. *Global feature importance based on the SHAP value*

Recipe 4-4. Explain a Random Forest Regressor with Global and Local Interpretations

Problem

Random forest (RF) is a bagging approach to create ensemble models; it is also difficult to interpret which tree generated the final prediction and interpret the global and local interpretations.

Solution

We are going to use the tree explainer from the SHAP library.

How It Works

Let's take a look at the following example:

```
import shap
from sklearn.ensemble import RandomForestRegressor
rforest = RandomForestRegressor(n_estimators=100, max_depth=3,
min_samples_split=20, random_state=0)
rforest.fit(X, y)

# explain all the predictions in the test set
explainer = shap.TreeExplainer(rforest)
shap_values = explainer.shap_values(X)

shap.summary_plot(shap_values, X)
```

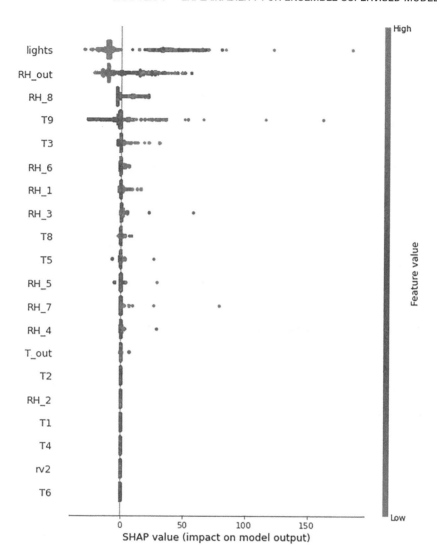

Figure 4-11. *SHAP value impact on model prediction*

```
shap.dependence_plot("lights", shap_values, X)
```

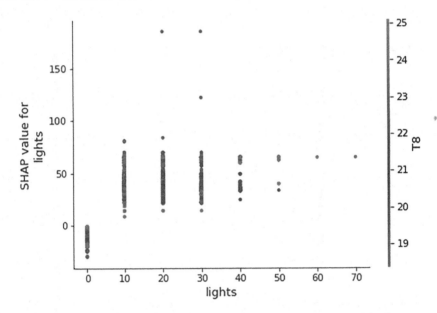

Figure 4-12. *SHAP value of lights plotted against T8 and lights*

```
# explain all the predictions in the dataset
shap.force_plot(explainer.expected_value, shap_values, X)

shap.partial_dependence_plot(
    "lights", rforest.predict, X, ice=False,
    model_expected_value=True, feature_expected_value=True
)
```

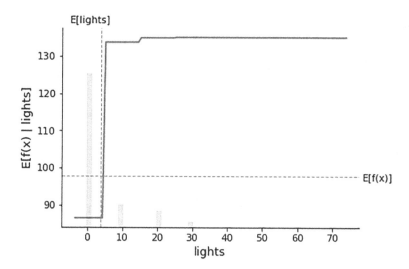

Figure 4-13. *Partial dependency plot of lights*

Recipe 4-5. Explain the Catboost Regressor with Global and Local Interpretations

Problem

Catboost is another model that fasten the model training process by explicitly declaring the categorical features. If there is no categorical feature, then the model is trained on all numeric features as well. You want to explain the global and local interpretations from the catboost regression model.

Solution

We are going to use the tree explainer from the SHAP library and the catboost library.

How It Works

Let's take a look at the following example:

```
!pip install catboost
import catboost
from catboost import *
import shap
shap.initjs()

model = CatBoostRegressor(iterations=100, learning_rate=0.1,
random_seed=123)
model.fit(X, y, verbose=False, plot=False)

explainer = shap.TreeExplainer(model)
shap_values = explainer.shap_values(X)

# summarize the effects of all the features
shap.summary_plot(shap_values, X)
```

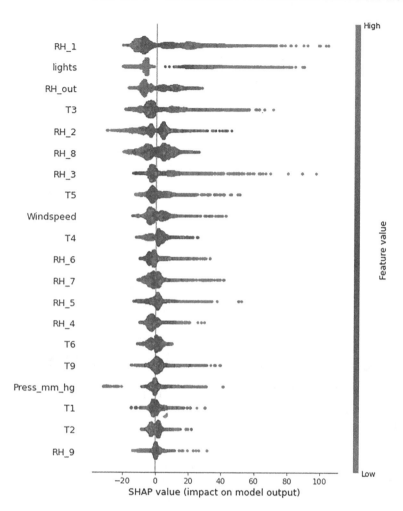

Figure 4-14. *SHAP value impact on model predictions*

```
# create a SHAP dependence plot to show the effect of a single
feature across the whole dataset
shap.dependence_plot("lights", shap_values, X)
```

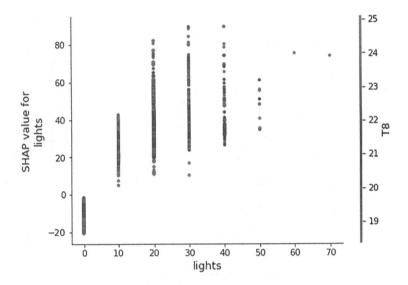

Figure 4-15.   *SHAP value of lights dependence plot*

Recipe 4-6. Explain the EBM Classifier with Global and Local Interpretations

Problem

EBM is an explainable boosting machine for a classifier. You want to explain the global and local interpretations from the EBM classifier model.

Solution

We are going to use the tree explainer from the SHAP library.

How It Works

Let's take a look at the following example. We are going to use a public automobile dataset with some modifications. The objective is to predict the price of a vehicle given the features such as make, location, age, etc. It is a regression problem that we are going to solve using a mix of numeric and categorical features.

```
df = pd.read_csv('https://raw.githubusercontent.com/
pradmishra1/PublicDatasets/main/automobile.csv')
df.head(3)
df.columns
Index(['Price', 'Make', 'Location', 'Age', 'Odometer',
'FuelType', 'Transmission', 'OwnerType', 'Mileage', 'EngineCC',
'PowerBhp'], dtype='object')
```

We cannot use the string-based features or categorical features in the model directly because matrix multiplication is not possible on string features; hence, the string-based features need to be transformed into dummy variables or binary features with 0 and 1 flags. The transformation step is skipped here as many data scientists already know how to do data transformation. We are importing another transformed dataset directly.

```
df_t = pd.read_csv('https://raw.githubusercontent.com/
pradmishra1/PublicDatasets/main/Automobile_transformed.csv')
del df_t['Unnamed: 0']
df_t.head(3)
df_t.columns
Index(['Price', 'Age', 'Odometer', 'mileage', 'engineCC',
'powerBhp', 'Location_Bangalore', 'Location_Chennai',
'Location_Coimbatore', 'Location_Delhi', 'Location_Hyderabad',
'Location_Jaipur', 'Location_Kochi', 'Location_Kolkata',
'Location_Mumbai', 'Location_Pune', 'FuelType_Diesel',
'FuelType_Electric', 'FuelType_LPG', 'FuelType_Petrol',
```

```
'Transmission_Manual', 'OwnerType_Fourth +ACY- Above',
'OwnerType_Second', 'OwnerType_Third'], dtype='object')

#y is the dependent variable, that we need to predict
y = df_t.pop('Price')
# X is the set of input features
X = df_t

from interpret import set_visualize_provider
from interpret.provider import InlineProvider
set_visualize_provider(InlineProvider())

import pandas as pd
from sklearn.model_selection import train_test_split

from interpret.glassbox import ExplainableBoostingClassifier
from interpret import show

import shap
import sklearn
```

To compute the SHAP values, we can use the explainer function with the training dataset X and the model predict function. The SHAP value calculation takes place using a permutation approach; it took 5 minutes.

```
# fit a GAM model to the data
import interpret.glassbox
import shap
model_ebm = interpret.glassbox.ExplainableBoostingRegressor()
model_ebm.fit(X, y)

X100 = X[:100]

# explain the GAM model with SHAP
explainer_ebm = shap.Explainer(model_ebm.predict, X100)
shap_values_ebm = explainer_ebm(X100)
```

```
import numpy as np
pd.DataFrame(np.round(shap_values_ebm.values,2)).head(2)

pd.DataFrame(np.round(shap_values_ebm.base_values,2)).head(2)
```

Recipe 4-7. SHAP Partial Dependency Plot for Regression Models with Mixed Input

Problem

You want to plot the partial dependency plot and interpret the graph for numeric and categorical dummy variables.

Solution

The partial dependency plot shows the correlation between a feature and the predicted output of the target variables. There are two ways we can showcase the results, one with a feature and expected value of the prediction function and the other by superimposing a data point on the partial dependency plot.

How It Works

Let's take a look at the following example:

```
from interpret import set_visualize_provider
from interpret.provider import InlineProvider
set_visualize_provider(InlineProvider())
from interpret import show
ebm_global = model_ebm.explain_global()
show(ebm_global)
```

```
ebm_local = model_ebm.explain_local(X[:5], y[:5])
show(ebm_local)

# make a standard partial dependence plot with a single SHAP
value overlaid
sample_ind = 20
fig,ax = shap.partial_dependence_plot(
    "powerBhp", model_ebm.predict, X100, model_expected_
    value=True,
    feature_expected_value=True, show=False, ice=False,
    shap_values=shap_values_ebm[sample_ind:sample_ind+1,:]
)
```

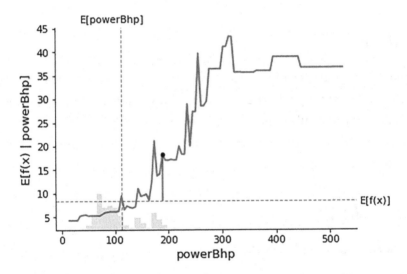

Figure 4-16. *Nonlinear relationship between the powerBhp and the predicted output from the model*

The nonlinear blue line shows the positive correlation between the price and the powerBhp. The powerBhp is a strong feature; the higher the bhp, the higher the price of the car.

```
shap.partial_dependence_plot(
    "powerBhp", model_ebm.predict, X, ice=False,
    model_expected_value=True, feature_expected_value=True
)
```

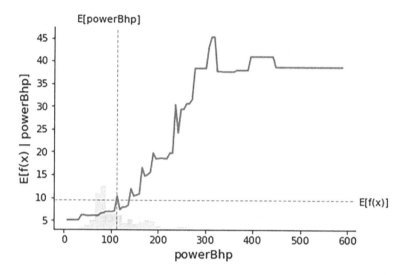

Figure 4-17. *Partial dependence plot of powerBhp*

This is a continuous or numeric feature. Let's look at the binary or dummy features. There are two dummy features for if the car is registered in Bangalore or in Kolkata.

```
shap.partial_dependence_plot(
    "Location_Bangalore", model_ebm.predict, X, ice=False,
    model_expected_value=True, feature_expected_value=True
)
```

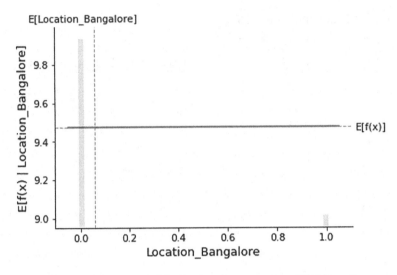

Figure 4-18. *Dummy variable Bangalore versus SHAP value*

If the location of the car is Bangalore, then the price will be 9.5, and it remains constant.

```
shap.partial_dependence_plot(
    "Location_Kolkata", model_ebm.predict, X, ice=False,
    model_expected_value=True, feature_expected_value=True
)
```

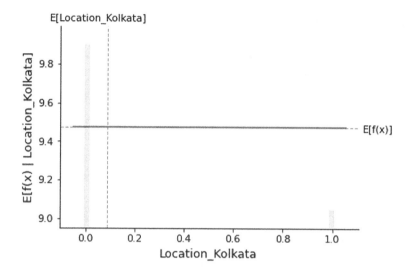

Figure 4-19. *Dummy variable Location_Kolkata versus SHAP value*

If the location is Kolkata, then the price is expected to be the same. There is no impact of the dummy variable on the price.

Recipe 4-8. SHAP Feature Importance for Tree Regression Models with Mixed Input Variables

Problem

You want to get the global feature importance from SHAP values using mixed input feature data.

Solution

The solution to this problem is to use absolute values, sort them in descending order, and populate them in waterfall chart, beeswarm chart, scatter plot, etc.

How It Works

Let's take a look at the following example:

```
shap.plots.scatter(shap_values_ebm[:,"powerBhp"])
```

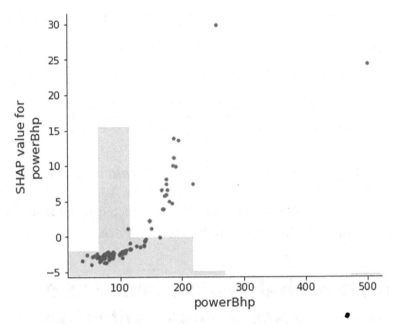

Figure 4-20. *Scatter plot of powerBhp and its SHAP values*

```
# the waterfall_plot shows how we get from explainer.expected_
value to model.predict(X)[sample_ind]
shap.plots.waterfall(shap_values_ebm[sample_ind],
max_display=14)
```

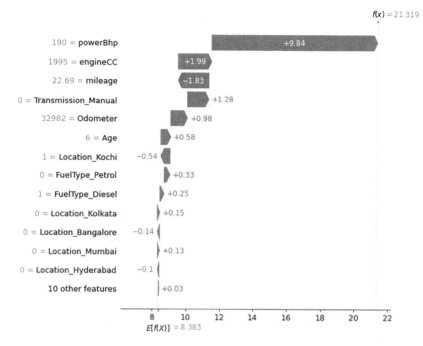

Figure 4-21. *Feature importance for a specific example*

```
# the waterfall_plot shows how we get from explainer.expected_
value to model.predict(X)[sample_ind]
shap.plots.beeswarm(shap_values_ebm, max_display=14)
```

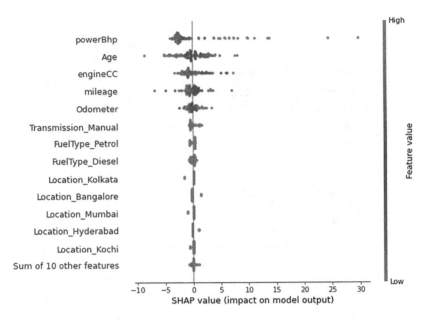

Figure 4-22. *Importance of SHAP values on model prediction*

```
# explain all the predictions in the dataset
shap.summary_plot(shap_values_ebm, X100)
```

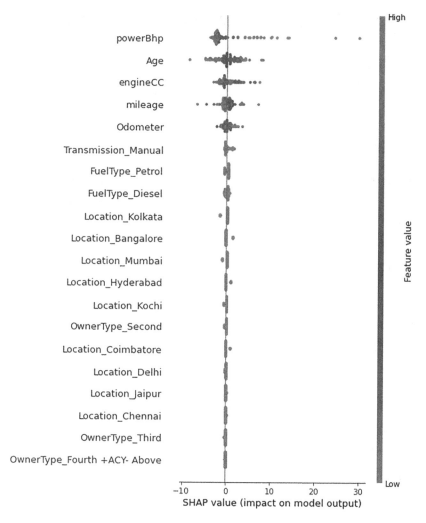

Figure 4-23. *Explaining all predictions with feature importance*

At a high level, for the tree-based nonlinear model that is used to predict the price of the automobiles, the previous features are important. The highest is the powerBhp, age of the car, petrol type, manual transmission type, etc. The previous tabular output shows the global feature importance.

Recipe 4-9. Explaining the XGBoost Model

Problem

You want to generate explainability for an XGBoost model for regression.

Solution

The XGBoost regressor trained on 100 trees and with a max depth parameter of 3 using a dataset that contains both numerical and categorial features. The total number of features are 23; an ideal dataset for XGBoost would be where we have more than 50 features. However, that requires more computation time.

How It Works

Let's take a look at the following example:

```
# train XGBoost model
import xgboost
model_xgb = xgboost.XGBRegressor(n_estimators=100, max_
depth=2).fit(X, y)

# explain the GAM model with SHAP
explainer_xgb = shap.Explainer(model_xgb, X)
shap_values_xgb = explainer_xgb(X)

# make a standard partial dependence plot with a single SHAP
value overlaid
sample_ind = 18
fig,ax = shap.partial_dependence_plot(
    "powerBhp", model_xgb.predict, X, model_expected_
    value=True,
```

```
            feature_expected_value=True, show=False, ice=False,
            shap_values=shap_values_xgb[sample_ind:sample_ind+1,:]
)
```

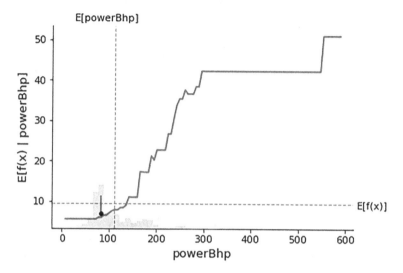

Figure 4-24. *Partial dependency plot with a sample*

```
shap.plots.scatter(shap_values_xgb[:,"mileage"])
```

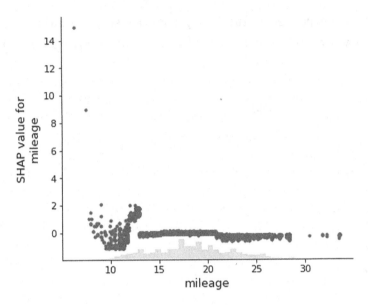

Figure 4-25. *Mileage feature and its SHAP values*

```
shap.plots.scatter(shap_values_xgb[:,"powerBhp"], color=shap_
values_xgb)
```

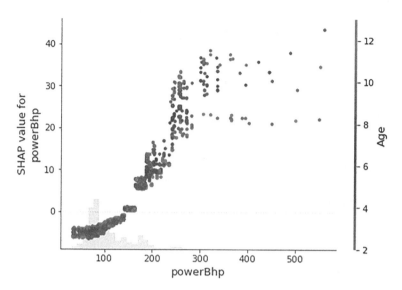

Figure 4-26. *Scatter plot of powerBhp, age, and SHAP value of powerBhp*

```
shap.summary_plot(shap_values_xgb, X)
```

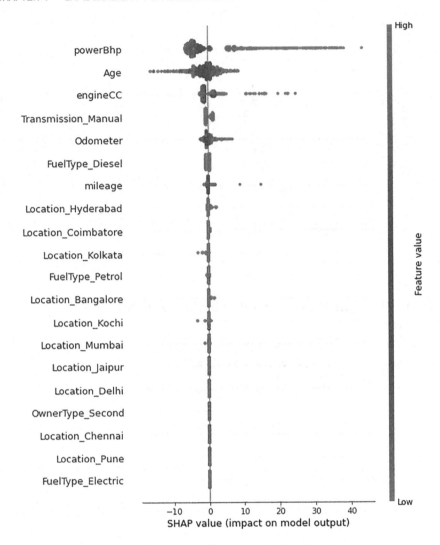

Figure 4-27. *SHAP value impact on model predictions*

Recipe 4-10. Random Forest Regressor for Mixed Data Types

Problem

You want to generate explainability for a random forest model using numeric as well as categorical features.

Solution

Random forest is useful when we have more features, say, more than 50; however, for this recipe, it is applied on 23 features. We could pick up a large dataset, but that would require more computations and may take more time to train. So, be cognizant about the model configurations when the model is being trained on a smaller machine.

How It Works

Let's take a look at the following example:

```
import shap
from sklearn.ensemble import RandomForestRegressor
rforest = RandomForestRegressor(n_estimators=100, max_depth=3,
min_samples_split=20, random_state=0)
rforest.fit(X, y)

# explain all the predictions in the test set
explainer = shap.TreeExplainer(rforest)
shap_values = explainer.shap_values(X)

shap.summary_plot(shap_values, X)
```

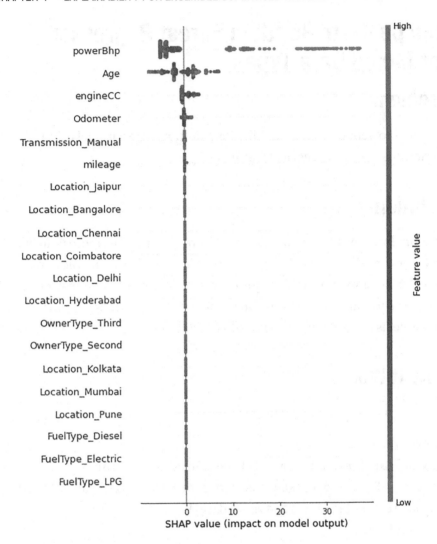

Figure 4-28. *SHAP value impact on model output*

```
shap.dependence_plot("powerBhp", shap_values, X)
```

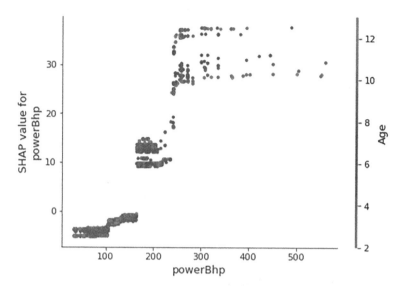

Figure 4-29. *SHAP dependence plot*

```
shap.partial_dependence_plot(
    "mileage", rforest.predict, X, ice=False,
    model_expected_value=True, feature_expected_value=True
)
```

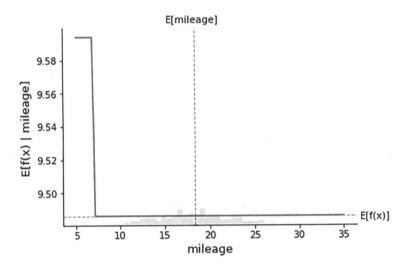

Figure 4-30.   *Partial dependency plot of mileage*

Recipe 4-11. Explaining the Catboost Model

Problem

You want to generate explainability for a dataset where most of the features are categorical. We can use a boosting model where a lot of variables are categorical.

Solution

The catboost model is known to work when we have more categorical variables compared to numeric variables. Hence, we can use the catboost regressor.

How It Works

Let's take a look at the following example:

```
!pip install catboost
import catboost
from catboost import *
import shap

model = CatBoostRegressor(iterations=100, learning_rate=0.1,
random_seed=123)
model.fit(X, y, verbose=False, plot=False)
explainer = shap.TreeExplainer(model)
shap_values = explainer.shap_values(X)

# summarize the effects of all the features
shap.summary_plot(shap_values, X)
```

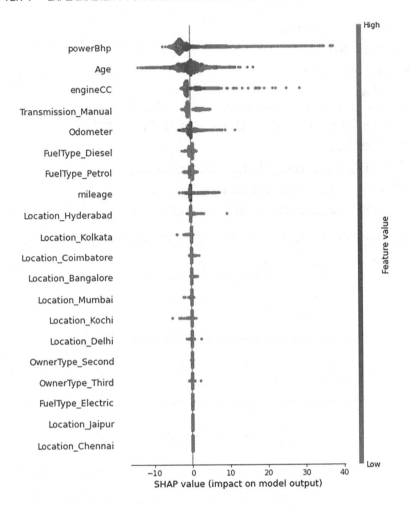

Figure 4-31. *SHAP value impact on model predictions*

```
# create a SHAP dependence plot to show the effect of a single
feature across the whole dataset
shap.dependence_plot("powerBhp", shap_values, X)
```

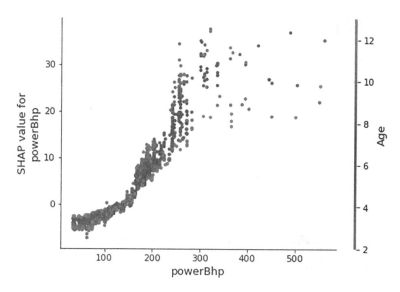

Figure 4-32. *SHAP dependence plot*

Recipe 4-12. LIME Explainer for the Catboost Model and Tabular Data

Problem

You want to generate explainability at a local level in a focused manner rather than at a global level.

Solution

The solution to this problem is to use the LIME library. LIME is a model-agnostic technique; it retrains the ML model while running the explainer. LIME localizes a problem and explains the model at a local level.

165

How It Works

Let's take a look at the following example. LIME requires a numpy array as an input to the tabular explainer; hence, the Pandas dataframe needs to be transformed into an array.

```
!pip install lime
Looking in indexes: https://pypi.org/simple, https://us-python.
pkg.dev/colab-wheels/public/simple/
Collecting lime
  Downloading lime-0.2.0.1.tar.gz (275 kB)
     |███████████████████████████████████████
██████████████████████| 275 kB 3.9 MB/s
Requirement already satisfied: matplotlib in /usr/local/lib/
python3.7/dist-packages (from lime) (3.2.2)
Requirement already satisfied: numpy in /usr/local/lib/
python3.7/dist-packages (from lime) (1.21.6)
Requirement already satisfied: scipy in /usr/local/lib/
python3.7/dist-packages (from lime) (1.7.3)
Require
. . . . . . . . . . . . . . .
import lime
import lime.lime_tabular

explainer = lime.lime_tabular.LimeTabularExplainer(np.array(X),
                                         mode=
                                         'regression',
                                         feature_names=X.
                                         columns,
                                         class_
                                         names=['price'],
                                         verbose=True)
```

We are using the energy prediction data from this chapter only.

```
explainer.feature_selection

# asking for explanation for LIME model
i = 60
exp = explainer.explain_instance(np.array(X)[i],
                                 model.predict,
                                 num_features=14
                                 )

model.predict(X)[60]


X[60:61]
Intercept 2.412781377314505
Prediction_local [26.44019841]
Right: 18.91681746836109

exp.show_in_notebook(show_table=True)
```

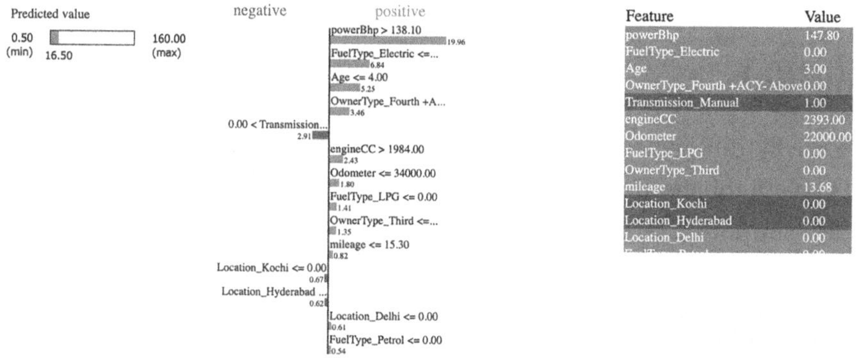

Figure 4-33. *Local explanation for the 60th record from the dataset*

```
[('powerBhp > 138.10', 11.685972887206468), ('Age <=
4.00', 5.069171125183003), ('engineCC > 1984.00',
3.2307037317922287), ('0.00 < Transmission_Manual <=
1.00', -2.175314285519644), ('Odometer <= 34000.00',
```

```
2.0903883419638976), ('OwnerType_Fourth +ACY- Above <=
0.00', 1.99286243362804), ('Location_Hyderabad <= 0.00',
-1.4395857770864107), ('mileage <= 15.30', 1.016369130009493),
('0.00 < FuelType_Diesel <= 1.00', 0.8477072936504322),
('Location_Kolkata <= 0.00', 0.6908993069146472), ('FuelType_
Petrol <= 0.00', 0.654629068871846), ('Location_Bangalore
<= 0.00', -0.47395963805113284), ('FuelType_Electric <=
0.00', 0.4285429019735695), ('Location_Delhi <= 0.00',
0.40903051200940277)]
```

Recipe 4-13. ELI5 Explainer for Tabular Data

Problem

You want to use the ELI5 library for generating explanations of a linear regression model.

Solution

ELI5 is a Python package that helps to debug a machine learning model and explain the predictions. It provides support for all machine learning models supported by the scikit-learn library.

How It Works

Let's take a look at the following example:

```
pip install eli5
import eli5
eli5.show_weights(model,
                  feature_names=list(X.columns))
```

Weight	Feature
0.4385	powerBhp
0.2572	Age
0.0976	engineCC
0.0556	Odometer
0.0489	Mileage
0.0396	Transmission_Manual
0.0167	FuelType_Petrol
0.0165	FuelType_Diesel
0.0104	Location_Hyderabad
0.0043	Location_Coimbatore
0.0043	Location_Kolkata
0.0035	Location_Kochi
0.0025	Location_Bangalore
0.0021	Location_Mumbai
0.0014	Location_Delhi
0.0006	OwnerType_Third
0.0003	OwnerType_Second
0.0000	FuelType_Electric
0	OwnerType_Fourth +ACY- Above
0	Location_Pune

```
eli5.explain_weights(model, feature_names=list(X.columns))
```

Weight	Feature
0.4385	powerBhp
0.2572	Age
0.0976	engineCC
0.0556	Odometer
0.0489	Mileage
0.0396	Transmission_Manual
0.0167	FuelType_Petrol
0.0165	FuelType_Diesel
0.0104	Location_Hyderabad
0.0043	Location_Coimbatore
0.0043	Location_Kolkata
0.0035	Location_Kochi
0.0025	Location_Bangalore
0.0021	Location_Mumbai
0.0014	Location_Delhi
0.0006	OwnerType_Third
0.0003	OwnerType_Second
0.0000	FuelType_Electric
0	OwnerType_Fourth +ACY- Above
0	Location_Pune

```
from eli5.sklearn import PermutationImportance

perm = PermutationImportance(model)
perm.fit(X, y)
eli5.show_weights(perm,feature_names=list(X.columns))
```

Weight	Feature
0.6743 ± 0.0242	powerBhp
0.2880 ± 0.0230	Age
0.1188 ± 0.0068	engineCC
0.0577 ± 0.0028	Transmission_Manual
0.0457 ± 0.0048	Odometer
0.0354 ± 0.0053	mileage
0.0134 ± 0.0018	Location_Hyderabad
0.0082 ± 0.0022	FuelType_Petrol
0.0066 ± 0.0013	FuelType_Diesel
0.0042 ± 0.0010	Location_Kochi
0.0029 ± 0.0006	Location_Kolkata
0.0023 ± 0.0010	Location_Coimbatore
0.0017 ± 0.0002	Location_Bangalore
0.0014 ± 0.0005	Location_Mumbai
0.0014 ± 0.0006	Location_Delhi
0.0007 ± 0.0001	OwnerType_Third
0.0002 ± 0.0000	OwnerType_Second
0.0000 ± 0.0000	FuelType_Electric
0 ± 0.0000	Location_Chennai
0 ± 0.0000	FuelType_LPG

The results table has a BIAS value as a feature. This can be interpreted as an intercept term for a linear regression model. Other features are listed based on their descending order of importance based on their weight. The show weights function provides a global interpretation of the model, and the show prediction function provides local interpretation by taking into account a record from the training set.

Recipe 4-14. How the Permutation Model in ELI5 Works

Problem

You want to make sense of the ELI5 permutation library.

Solution

The solution to this problem is to use a dataset and a trained model.

How It Works

The permutation model in the ELI5 library works only for global interpretation. First it takes a baseline model from the training dataset and computes the error of the model. Then it shuffles the values of a feature, retrains the model, and computes the error. It compares the decrease in error after shuffling and before shuffling. A feature can be considered as important if after shuffling the error delta is high, and unimportant if the error delta is low. The result displays the average importance of features and the standard deviation of features with multiple shuffle steps.

Recipe 4-15. Global Explanation for Ensemble Classification Models

Problem

You want to explain the predictions generated from a classification model using ensemble models.

Solution

The logistic regression model is also known as a classification model as we model the probabilities from either a binary classification or a multinomial classification variable. In this particular recipe, we are using a churn classification dataset that has two outcomes: whether the customer is likely to churn or not. Let's use the ensemble models such as the explainable boosting machine for the classifier, extreme gradient boosting classifier, random forest classifier, and catboost classifier.

How It Works

Let's take a look at the following example. The key is to get the SHAP values, which will return base values, SHAP values, and data. Using the SHAP values we can create various explanations using graphs and figures. The SHAP values are always at a global level.

```
import pandas as pd
import numpy as np
import matplotlib.pyplot as plt
%matplotlib inline
from sklearn import tree, metrics, model_selection,
preprocessing
```

173

```
from sklearn.metrics import confusion_matrix,
classification_report

df_train = pd.read_csv('https://raw.githubusercontent.com/
pradmishra1/PublicDatasets/main/ChurnData_test.csv')
from sklearn.preprocessing import LabelEncoder

tras = LabelEncoder()
df_train['area_code_tr'] = tras.fit_transform(df_
train['area_code'])
df_train.columns
del df_train['area_code']
df_train.columns
df_train['target_churn_dum'] = pd.get_dummies(df_train.
churn,prefix='churn',drop_first=True)
df_train.columns
del df_train['international_plan']
del df_train['voice_mail_plan']
del df_train['churn']
df_train.info()
del df_train['Unnamed: 0']
df_train.columns
from sklearn.model_selection import train_test_split

X = df_train[['account_length', 'number_vmail_messages',
'total_day_minutes',
        'total_day_calls', 'total_day_charge', 'total_eve_
        minutes',
        'total_eve_calls', 'total_eve_charge', 'total_night_
        minutes',
        'total_night_calls', 'total_night_charge', 'total_intl_
        minutes',
        'total_intl_calls', 'total_intl_charge',
```

```
            'number_customer_service_calls', 'area_code_tr']]
Y = df_train['target_churn_dum']

import pandas as pd
from sklearn.model_selection import train_test_split

from interpret.glassbox import ExplainableBoostingClassifier
from interpret import show

xtrain,xtest,ytrain,ytest=train_test_split(X,Y,test_
size=0.20,stratify=Y)
ebm = ExplainableBoostingClassifier(random_state=12)
ebm.fit(xtrain, ytrain)

ebm_global = ebm.explain_global()
show(ebm_global)

ebm_local = ebm.explain_local(xtest[:5], ytest[:5])
show(ebm_local)

print("training accuracy:", ebm.score(xtrain,ytrain)) #training
accuracy

print("test accuracy:",ebm.score(xtest,ytest)) # test accuracy

show(ebm_global)

from interpret import set_visualize_provider
from interpret.provider import InlineProvider
set_visualize_provider(InlineProvider())
from interpret import show

X100 = X[:100]

# explain the GAM model with SHAP
explainer_ebm = shap.Explainer(ebm.predict, X100)
shap_values_ebm = explainer_ebm(X100)
```

```
ebm_global = ebm.explain_global()
show(ebm_global)

import numpy as np
pd.DataFrame(np.round(shap_values_ebm.values,2)).head(2)
```

Recipe 4-16. Partial Dependency Plot for a Nonlinear Classifier

Problem

You want to show feature associations with the class probabilities using a nonlinear classifier.

Solution

The class probabilities in this example are related to predicting the probability of churn. The SHAP value for a feature can be plotted against the feature value to show a scatter chart that displays the correlation, positive or negative, and the strength of associations.

How It Works

Let's take a look at the following example:

```
# make a standard partial dependence plot with a single SHAP
value overlaid
sample_ind = 20
fig,ax = shap.partial_dependence_plot(
    "number_customer_service_calls", ebm.predict, X100, model_
    expected_value=True,
    feature_expected_value=True, show=False, ice=False,
```

```
    shap_values=shap_values_ebm[sample_ind:sample_ind+1,:]
)
```

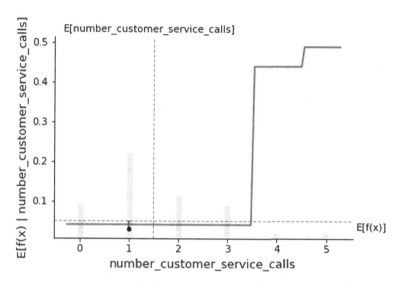

Figure 4-34. *Account length and SHAP value of account length*

```
# make a standard partial dependence plot with a single SHAP
value overlaid
sample_ind = 20
fig,ax = shap.partial_dependence_plot(
    "number_vmail_messages", ebm.predict, X100, model_expected_
    value=True,
    feature_expected_value=True, show=False, ice=False,
    shap_values=shap_values_ebm[sample_ind:sample_ind+1,:]
)
```

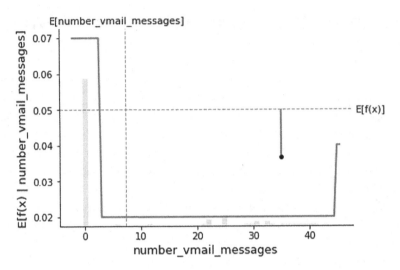

Figure 4-35. *Number of voicemail messages and SHAP values*

Recipe 4-17. Global Feature Importance from the Nonlinear Classifier

Problem

You want to get the global feature importance for the decision tree classification model.

Solution

The solution to this problem is to use the explainer log odds.

How It Works

Let's take a look at the following example:

```
shap.plots.scatter(shap_values_ebm)
```

178

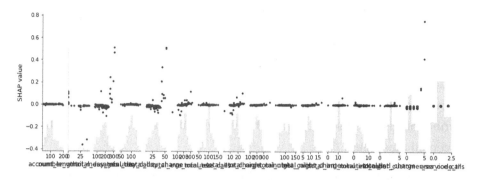

Figure 4-36. *All features SHAP values plotted together*

```
# the waterfall_plot shows how we get from explainer.expected_
value to model.predict(X)[sample_ind]
shap.plots.waterfall(shap_values_ebm[sample_ind], max_
display=14)
```

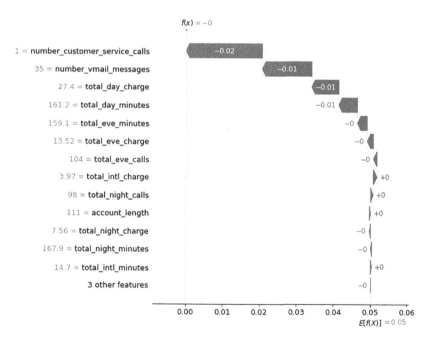

Figure 4-37. *Local explanation for record 20*

The interpretation goes like this: when we change the value of a feature by 1 unit, the model equation will produce two odds; one is the base, and the other is the incremental value of the feature. We are looking at the ratio of odds changes with every increase or decrease in the value of a feature. From the global feature importance, there are three important features: the number of customer service calls, the total day minutes, and the number of voicemail messages.

```
# the waterfall_plot shows how we get from explainer.expected_
value to model.predict(X)[sample_ind]
shap.plots.beeswarm(shap_values_ebm, max_display=14)
```

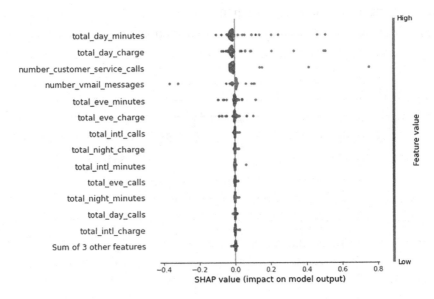

Figure 4-38. *SHAP values from EBM model on model predictions*

Recipe 4-18. XGBoost Model Explanation

Problem

You want to explain an extreme gradient boosting model, which is a sequential boosting model.

Solution

The model explanation can be done using SHAP; however, one of the limitations of SHAP is we cannot use the full data to create global and local explanations. We will take a subset if the smaller machine is allocated and a full dataset if the machine configuration supports it.

How It Works

Let's take a look at the following example:

```
# train XGBoost model
import xgboost
model = xgboost.XGBClassifier(n_estimators=100, max_depth=2).
fit(X, Y)

# compute SHAP values
explainer = shap.Explainer(model, X)
shap_values = explainer(X)

# make a standard partial dependence plot with a single SHAP
value overlaid
sample_ind = 18
fig,ax = shap.partial_dependence_plot(
    "account_length", model.predict, X, model_expected_
    value=True,
```

```
    feature_expected_value=True, show=False, ice=False,
    shap_values=shap_values_xgb[sample_ind:sample_ind+1,:]
)
```

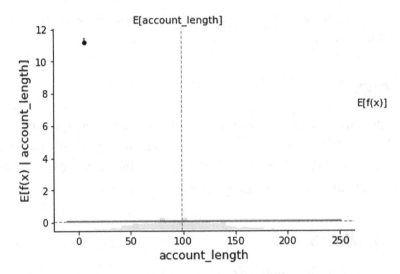

Figure 4-39. *Partial dependency plot for 18th record from training dataset*

```
import numpy as np
pd.DataFrame(np.round(shap_values.values,2)).head(2)
```

```
# the waterfall_plot shows how we get from explainer.expected_
value to model.predict(X)[sample_ind]
shap.plots.waterfall(shap_values[sample_ind], max_display=14)
```

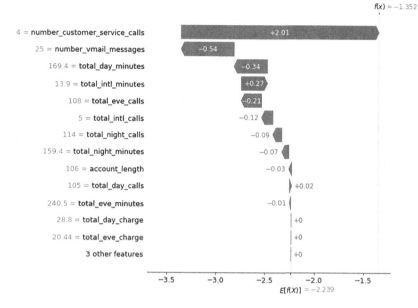

Figure 4-40. *Local explanation for 18th record*

```
# the waterfall_plot shows how we get from explainer.expected_
value to model.predict(X)[sample_ind]
shap.plots.scatter(shap_values[:,"account_length"])
```

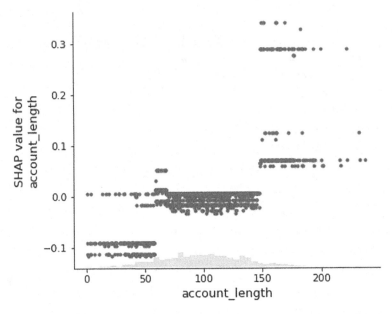

Figure 4-41. *Distribution of account length versus SHAP values*

```
# the waterfall_plot shows how we get from explainer.expected_
value to model.predict(X)[sample_ind]
shap.plots.scatter(shap_values[:,"number_vmail_messages"])
```

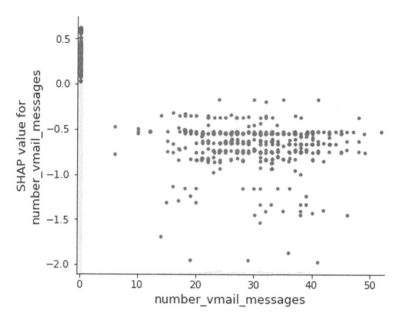

Figure 4-42. *Distribution of number of voicemail messages versus its SHAP values*

```
# the waterfall_plot shows how we get from explainer.expected_
value to model.predict(X)[sample_ind]
shap.plots.beeswarm(shap_values, max_display=14)
```

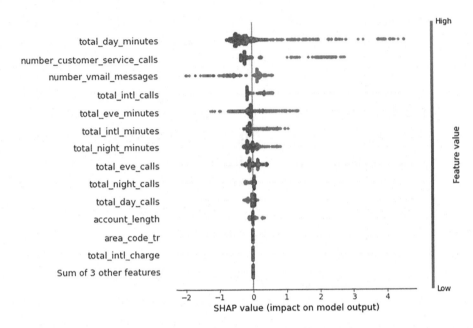

Figure 4-43. *SHAP value impact on model output*

```
shap.plots.bar(shap_values)
```

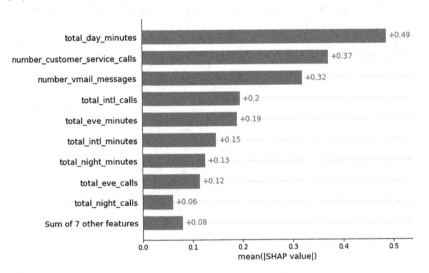

Figure 4-44. *Absolute average SHAP values shows importance of features*

```
shap.plots.heatmap(shap_values[:5000])
```

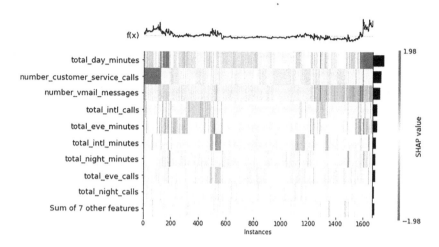

Figure 4-45. *Distribution of density of all features with their SHAP values*

```
shap.plots.scatter(shap_values[:,"total_day_minutes"])
```

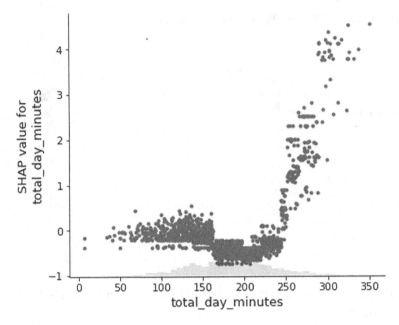

Figure 4-46. *Distribution of feature total day minutes with SHAP values*

```
shap.plots.scatter(shap_values[:,"total_day_minutes"],
color=shap_values[:,"account_length"])
```

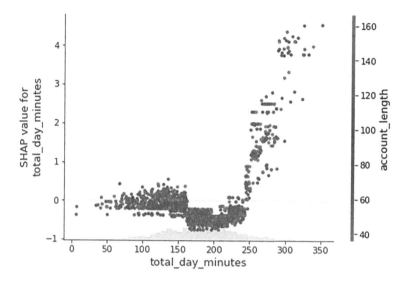

Figure 4-47. *Three-dimensional view of SHAP values*

Recipe 4-19. Explain a Random Forest Classifier

Problem

You want to get faster explanations from global and local explainable libraries using a random forest classifier. A random forest creates a family of trees as estimators and averages the predictions using the majority voting rule.

Solution

The model explanation can be done using SHAP; however, one of the limitations of SHAP is we cannot use the full data to create global and local explanations.

How It Works

Let's take a look at the following example:

```
import shap
from sklearn.ensemble import RandomForestClassifier
rforest = RandomForestClassifier(n_estimators=100, max_depth=3,
min_samples_split=20, random_state=0)
rforest.fit(X, Y)

# explain all the predictions in the test set
explainer = shap.TreeExplainer(rforest)
shap_values = explainer.shap_values(X)

shap.dependence_plot("account_length", shap_values[0], X)
```

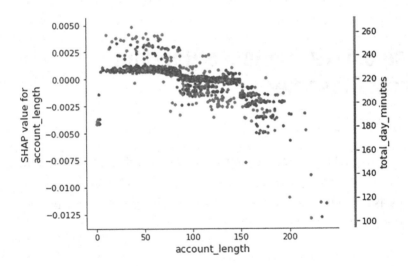

Figure 4-48. *Dependence plot from SHAP*

```
shap.partial_dependence_plot(
    "total_day_minutes", rforest.predict, X, ice=False,
    model_expected_value=True, feature_expected_value=True
)
```

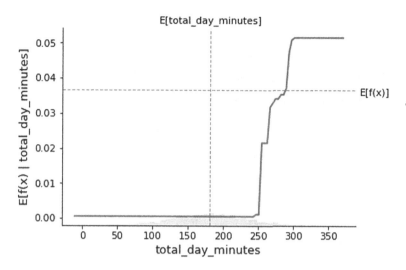

Figure 4-49. *Partial dependence plot of total day minutes*

```
shap.summary_plot(shap_values, X)
```

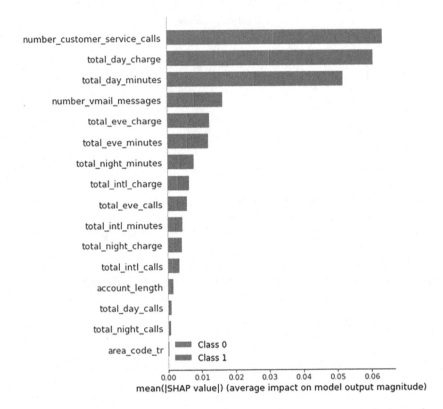

Figure 4-50. *Feature importance for two classes separately based on absolute average SHAP value*

Recipe 4-20. Catboost Model Interpretation for Classification Scenario

Problem

You want to get an explanation for the catboost model–based binary classification problem.

Solution

The model explanation can be done using SHAP; however, one of the limitations of SHAP is we cannot use the full data to create global and local explanations. Even if we decide to use the full data, it usually takes more time. Hence, to speed up the process of generating local and global explanations in a scenario when millions of records are being used to train a model, LIME is very useful. Catboost needs iterations to be defined.

How It Works

Let's take a look at the following example:

```
model = CatBoostClassifier(iterations=10, learning_rate=0.1,
random_seed=12)
model.fit(X, Y, verbose=True, plot=False)
0: learn: 0.6381393    total: 10.2ms    remaining: 91.9ms
1: learn: 0.5900921    total: 20.1ms    remaining: 80.2ms
2: learn: 0.5517727    total: 29.9ms    remaining: 69.8ms
3: learn: 0.5166202    total: 39.9ms    remaining: 59.9ms
4: learn: 0.4872410    total: 49.9ms    remaining: 49.9ms
5: learn: 0.4632012    total: 60.1ms    remaining: 40ms
6: learn: 0.4414588    total: 69.8ms    remaining: 29.9ms
7: learn: 0.4222780    total: 79.6ms    remaining: 19.9ms
8: learn: 0.4073681    total: 89.5ms    remaining: 9.95ms
9: learn: 0.3915051    total: 99.5ms    remaining: 0us

explainer = shap.TreeExplainer(model)
shap_values = explainer.shap_values(Pool(X, Y))
shap.force_plot(explainer.expected_value, shap_values[0,:],
X.iloc[0,:])
shap.force_plot(explainer.expected_value, shap_values[91,:],
X.iloc[91,:])
shap.summary_plot(shap_values, X)
```

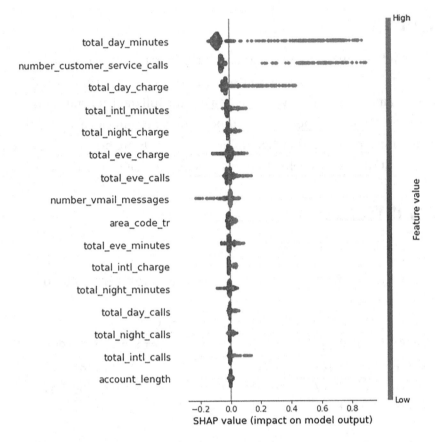

Figure 4-51. *SHAP value impact on model output*

Recipe 4-21. Local Explanations Using LIME

Problem

You want to get faster explanations from global and local explainable libraries.

Solution

The model explanation can be done using SHAP; however, one of the limitations of SHAP is we cannot use the full data to create global and local explanations. Even if we decide to use the full data, it usually takes more time. Hence, to speed up the process of generating local and global explanations in a scenario when millions of records are being used to train a model, LIME is very useful.

How It Works

Let's take a look at the following example:

```
import lime
import lime.lime_tabular

explainer = lime.lime_tabular.LimeTabularExplainer(np.
array(xtrain),

                   feature_names=list(xtrain.columns),
                   class_names=['target_churn_dum'],
                   verbose=True, mode='classification')

# this record is a no churn scenario
exp = explainer.explain_instance(X.iloc[0], model.predict_
proba, num_features=16)
exp.as_list()
Intercept 0.2758028503306529
Prediction_local [0.34562036]
Right: 0.23860629814459952
[('number_customer_service_calls > 2.00', 0.06944779279619419),
 ('total_day_minutes <= 144.10', -0.026032556397868205),
 ('area_code_tr > 1.00', 0.012192087473855579),
 ('total_day_charge <= 24.50', -0.01049348495191592),
```

```
('total_night_charge > 10.57', 0.009208937152255816),
('total_eve_calls <= 88.00', 0.007763649795450518),
('17.12 < total_eve_charge <= 19.74', 0.006648493070415344),
('number_vmail_messages <= 0.00', 0.0054214568436186375),
('98.00 < account_length <= 126.00', 0.004192090777110732),
('2.81 < total_intl_charge <= 3.21', -0.004030006982470514),
('201.40 < total_eve_minutes <= 232.20',
-0.0039743556975642405),
('total_night_minutes > 234.80', 0.0035628982403953778),
('total_night_calls <= 86.00', 0.0029612465055136334),
('total_day_calls > 112.00', -0.0028523783898236925),
('total_intl_calls <= 3.00', -0.002506612124522332),
('10.40 < total_intl_minutes <= 11.90',
-0.0016917444417898933)]
```

```
exp.show_in_notebook(show_table=True)
```

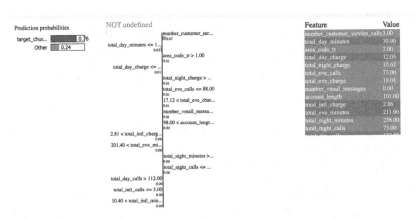

Figure 4-52. *Local explanation for record number 1 from test set*

```
# This is s churn scenario
exp = explainer.explain_instance(X.iloc[20], model.predict_
proba, num_features=16)
```

```
exp.as_list()
Intercept 0.32979383442829424
Prediction_local [0.22940692]
Right: 0.25256892775050466
[('number_customer_service_calls <= 1.00',
-0.03195279452926141),
 ('144.10 < total_day_minutes <= 181.00',
 -0.03105192670898253),
 ('total_intl_charge > 3.21', 0.010519683979779627),
 ('101.00 < total_eve_calls <= 114.00', -0.008871850152517477),
 ('0.00 < area_code_tr <= 1.00', -0.008355187259945206),
 ('total_intl_minutes > 11.90', 0.007391379556830906),
 ('24.50 < total_day_charge <= 30.77', -0.006975112181235882),
 ('total_night_charge <= 7.56', -0.006500647887830215),
 ('total_eve_charge <= 14.14', -0.006278552413626889),
 ('number_vmail_messages > 0.00', -0.0062185929677679875),
 ('total_night_minutes <= 167.90', -0.003079244107811434),
 ('4.00 < total_intl_calls <= 5.00', -0.0026984920221149998),
 ('total_day_calls > 112.00', -0.00247085902534  14045),
 ('total_eve_minutes <= 166.40', -0.002156339757484174),
 ('98.00 < account_length <= 126.00', -0.0013292154399683106),
 ('86.00 < total_night_calls <= 99.00', -0.00035916152353229)]
```

```
exp.show_in_notebook(show_table=True)
```

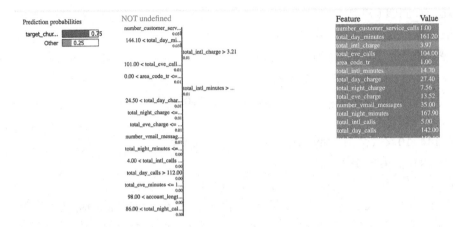

Figure 4-53. *Local explanations from 20th record from the test set*

In a similar fashion, the graphs can be generated for different records from the training set and test set, which are from the training sample as well as test sample.

Recipe 4-22. Model Explanations Using ELI5

Problem

You want to get model explanations using the ELI5 library.

Solution

ELI5 provides two functions, show weights and show predictions, to generate model explanations.

How It Works

Let's take a look at the following example:

```
eli5.show_weights(model,
                  feature_names=list(X.columns))
```

Weight	Feature
0.3703	total_day_minutes
0.2426	number_customer_service_calls
0.1181	total_day_charge
0.0466	total_eve_charge
0.0427	number_vmail_messages
0.0305	total_eve_minutes
0.0264	total_eve_calls
0.0258	total_intl_minutes
0.0190	total_night_minutes
0.0180	total_night_charge
0.0139	total_intl_charge
0.0133	area_code_tr
0.0121	total_day_calls
0.0110	total_intl_calls
0.0077	total_night_calls
0.0019	account_length

```
eli5.explain_weights(model, feature_names=list(X.columns))
```

Weight	Feature
0.3703	total_day_minutes
0.2426	number_customer_service_calls
0.1181	total_day_charge

(*continued*)

Weight	Feature
0.0466	total_eve_charge
0.0427	number_vmail_messages
0.0305	total_eve_minutes
0.0264	total_eve_calls
0.0258	total_intl_minutes
0.0190	total_night_minutes
0.0180	total_night_charge
0.0139	total_intl_charge
0.0133	area_code_tr
0.0121	total_day_calls
0.0110	total_intl_calls
0.0077	total_night_calls
0.0019	account_length

```
from eli5.sklearn import PermutationImportance
perm = PermutationImportance(model)
perm.fit(X,Y)
eli5.show_weights(perm,feature_names=list(X.columns))
```

Weight	Feature
0.0352 ± 0.0051	total_day_minutes
0.0250 ± 0.0006	total_day_charge
0.0121 ± 0.0024	number_vmail_messages
0.0110 ± 0.0051	total_eve_charge

(continued)

Weight	Feature
0.0052 ± 0.0048	total_night_minutes
0.0028 ± 0.0025	total_night_charge
0.0023 ± 0.0009	total_eve_calls
0.0022 ± 0.0012	number_customer_service_calls
0.0022 ± 0.0018	total_eve_minutes
0.0019 ± 0.0012	total_night_calls
0.0018 ± 0.0015	total_day_calls
0.0017 ± 0.0019	total_intl_minutes
0.0011 ± 0.0016	area_code_tr
0.0008 ± 0.0012	total_intl_charge
0.0005 ± 0.0018	total_intl_calls
-0.0010 ± 0.0018	account_length

Recipe 4-23. Multiclass Classification Model Explanation

Problem

You want to get model explanations for multiclass classification problems.

Solution

The expectation for multiclass classification is to first build a robust model with categorical features, if any, and explain the predictions. In a binary class classification problem, we can get the probabilities, and sometimes we can get the feature importance corresponding to each class from all kinds of ensemble models. Here is an example of a catboost model that can be used to generate the feature importance corresponding to each class in the multiclass classification problem.

How It Works

Let's take a look at the following example. We are going to use a dataset from the UCI ML repository. The URL to access the dataset is given in the following script:

```
import pandas as pd
df_red = pd.read_csv('https://archive.ics.uci.edu/ml/machine-
learning-databases/wine-quality/winequality-red.csv',sep=';')
df_white = pd.read_csv('https://archive.ics.uci.edu/ml/machine-
learning-databases/wine-quality/winequality-white.csv',sep=';')

features = ['fixed_acidity','volatile_acidity','citric_
acid','residual_sugar',
            'chlorides','free_sulfur_dioxide','total_sulfur_
            dioxide','density',
            'pH','sulphates','alcohol','quality']

df = pd.concat([df_red,df_white],axis=0)
df.columns = features
df.quality = pd.Categorical(df.quality)
df.head()

y = df.pop('quality')
X = df

import catboost
from catboost import *
import shap
shap.initjs()
```

```
model = CatBoostClassifier(loss_function = 'MultiClass',
                           iterations=300,
                           learning_rate=0.1,
                           random_seed=123)
model.fit(X, y, verbose=False, plot=False)

explainer = shap.TreeExplainer(model)
shap_values = explainer.shap_values(Pool(X, y))

set(y)
{3, 4, 5, 6, 7, 8, 9}

shap.summary_plot(shap_values[0], X)
```

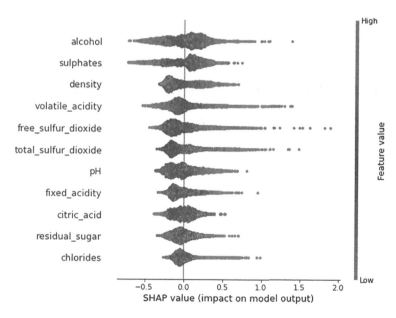

Figure 4-54. *SHAP value impact with respect to class 0 from the target variable*

```
shap.summary_plot(shap_values[1], X)
```

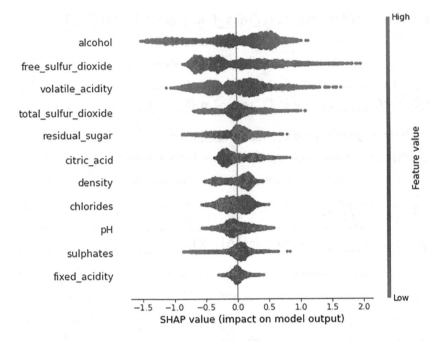

Figure 4-55. *SHAP summary plot for class 2 from the target variable*

```
shap.summary_plot(shap_values[2], X)
```

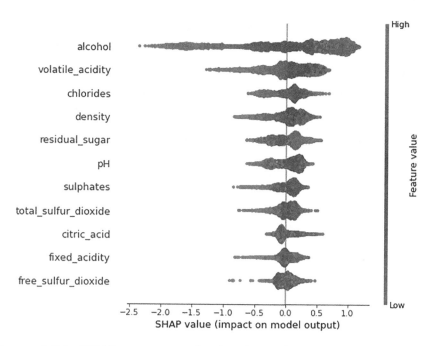

Figure 4-56. *SHAP summary plot for class 3 from the target variable*

Conclusion

In this chapter, we discussed the ensemble model explanations. The models we covered were explainable boosting regressor, explainable boosting classifier, extreme gradient boosting regressor and classifier, random forest regressor and classifier, and catboost classifier and regressor. The graphs and charts sometimes may look similar, but they are different, because of two reasons. First, the data points from SHAP that are available for plotting depend on the sample size selected to generate explanations. Second, the sample models are being trained with fewer iterations and with basic hyperparameters; hence, with a higher configuration machine, the full hyperparameter tuning can happen, and better SHAP values can be produced.

In the next chapter, we will cover the explainability for natural language–based tasks such as text classification and sentiment analysis and explain the predictions.

CHAPTER 5

Explainability for Natural Language Processing

Natural language processing tasks such as text classification and sentiment analysis can be explained using explainable AI libraries such as SHAP and ELI5. The objective of explaining the text classification tasks or sentiment analysis tasks is to let the user know how a decision was made. The predictions are generated using a supervised learning model for unstructured text data. The input is a text sentence or many sentences or phrases, and we train a machine learning model to perform text classification such as customer review classification, feedback classification, newsgroup classification, etc. In this chapter, we will be using explainable libraries to explain the predictions or classifications.

There are three common problems where explainability is required in natural language processing.

- Document classification, where the input is a series of sentences extracted from a document, and the output is the label attached to the document. If a document is misclassified or someone wants to know why a document is being classified by the algorithm in a certain way, we need to explain why.

© Pradeepta Mishra 2023
P. Mishra, *Explainable AI Recipes*, https://doi.org/10.1007/978-1-4842-9029-3_5

- For named entity recognition tasks, we need to predict the entity to which a name belongs. If it is assigned to another entity, we need to explain why.

- For sentiment analysis, if a sentiment category is wrongly assigned to another category, then we need to explain why.

Recipe 5-1. Explain Sentiment Analysis Text Classification Using SHAP

Problem

You want to explain sentiment analysis prediction using SHAP.

Solution

The solution takes into account the most common dataset available, which is the IMDB sentiment classification dataset from the SHAP library. It can be accessed using the SHAP dataset. We will be using the SHAP library to explain the predictions.

How It Works

Let's take a look at the following example (see Figure 5-1 and Figure 5-2):

```
!pip install shap
import warnings
warnings.filterwarnings("ignore")
import sklearn
from sklearn.feature_extraction.text import TfidfVectorizer
from sklearn.model_selection import train_test_split
```

```
import numpy as np
import shap

import pandas as pd
from keras.datasets import imdb

corpus,y = shap.datasets.imdb()
corpus_train, corpus_test, y_train, y_test = train_test_
split(corpus, y, test_size=0.2, random_state=7)

vectorizer = TfidfVectorizer(min_df=10)
X_train = vectorizer.fit_transform(corpus_train).toarray() #
sparse also works but Explanation slicing is not yet supported
X_test = vectorizer.transform(corpus_test).toarray()

corpus_train[20]
Well how was I suppose to know this was.....................
..........

y
array([False, False, False, ..., True, True, True])

model = sklearn.linear_model.LogisticRegression(penalty=
"l2", C=0.1)
model.fit(X_train, y_train)

explainer = shap.Explainer(model, X_train, feature_
names=vectorizer.get_feature_names())
shap_values = explainer(X_test)

shap.summary_plot(shap_values, X_test)
```

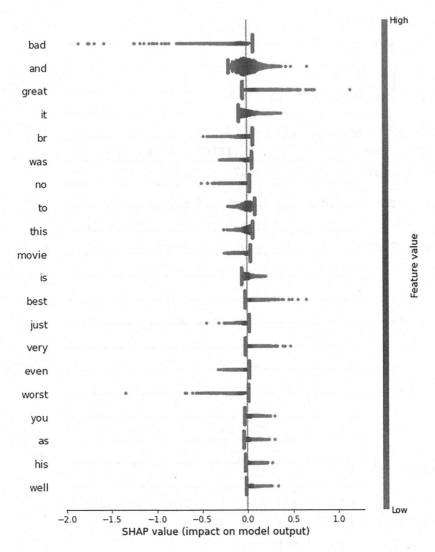

Figure 5-1. *Summary plot from sentiment classification*

```
shap.plots.beeswarm(shap_values)
```

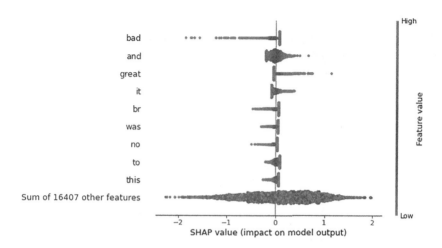

Figure 5-2. *SHAP values showing very sparse features*

```
names = vectorizer.get_feature_names()
names[0:20]
```

```
pd.DataFrame(X_train,columns=names)
```

	00	000	007	01	02	05	06	10	100	1000	...	zombi	zombie	zombies	zone	zoo	zoom	zooms	zorro	zu	zucker
0	0.0	0.0	0.0	0.0	0.0	0.0	0.0	0.0	0.000000	0.0	...	0.0	0.0	0.0	0.0	0.0	0.0	0.0	0.0	0.0	0.0
1	0.0	0.0	0.0	0.0	0.0	0.0	0.0	0.0	0.000000	0.0	...	0.0	0.0	0.0	0.0	0.0	0.0	0.0	0.0	0.0	0.0
2	0.0	0.0	0.0	0.0	0.0	0.0	0.0	0.0	0.000000	0.0	...	0.0	0.0	0.0	0.0	0.0	0.0	0.0	0.0	0.0	0.0
3	0.0	0.0	0.0	0.0	0.0	0.0	0.0	0.0	0.000000	0.0	...	0.0	0.0	0.0	0.0	0.0	0.0	0.0	0.0	0.0	0.0
4	0.0	0.0	0.0	0.0	0.0	0.0	0.0	0.0	0.078969	0.0	...	0.0	0.0	0.0	0.0	0.0	0.0	0.0	0.0	0.0	0.0

```
ind = 10
shap.plots.force(shap_values[ind])

print("Positive" if y_test[ind] else "Negative", "Review:")
print(corpus_test[ind])
Positive Review:
"Twelve Monkeys" is odd and disturbing, ......................
.................
```

Recipe 5-2. Explain Sentiment Analysis Text Classification Using ELI5

Problem

You want to explain sentiment analysis prediction using ELI5.

Solution

The solution takes into account the most common dataset available, which is the IMDB sentiment classification. We will be using the ELI5 library to explain the predictions.

How It Works

Let's take a look at the following example:

```
!pip install eli5
import eli5
eli5.show_weights(model, top=10) #this result is not
meaningful, as weight and feature names are not there
```

   y=True top features

Weight[?]	Feature
+3.069	x6530
+2.195	x748
+1.838	x1575
+1.788	x5270
+1.743	x8807
... 8173 more positive ...	
... 8234 more negative ...	
-1.907	x15924
-1.911	x1239
-2.027	x9976
-2.798	x16255
-3.643	x1283

The ELI5 results are not meaningful as they provide only the weights and features, and the feature names are not meaningful. To make the results interpretable, we need to pass the feature names.

```
eli5.show_weights(model,feature_names=vectorizer.get_feature_
names(),target_names=['Negative','Positive'])
#make sense
```

y=Positive top features

Weight[?]	Feature
+3.069	great
+2.195	and
+1.838	best
+1.788	excellent
+1.743	love
+1.501	well
+1.477	wonderful
+1.394	very

... 8170 more positive ...

... 8227 more negative ...

-1.391	just
-1.407	plot
-1.481	poor
-1.570	even
-1.589	terrible
-1.612	nothing
-1.723	boring
-1.907	waste
-1.911	awful
-2.027	no
-2.798	worst
-3.643	bad

Recipe 5-3. Local Explanation Using ELI5

Problem

You want to explain an individual review in the sentiment analysis prediction using ELI5.

Solution

The solution is takes into account the most common dataset available, which is the IMDB sentiment classification dataset. We will be using the ELI5 library to explain the predictions.

How It Works

Let's take a look at the following example. Here we are taking into account three reviews, record numbers 1, 20, and 100, to explain the predicted class and relative importance of each word contributing positively and negatively to the predicted class.

```
Eli5.show_prediction(model, corpus_train[3], vec=vectorizer,
                    target_names=['Negative','Positive'])
# explain local prediction
```

y=Positive (probability **0.739**, score **1.042**) top features

Contribution?	Feature
+0.869	Highlighted in text (sum)
+0.174	<BIAS>

as a matter of fact, this is one of those movies you would have to give 7.5 to. The fact is; as already stated, it's a great deal of fun. Wonderfully atmospheric. Askey does indeed come across as over the top, but it's a great vehicle for him, just as oh, mr porter is for will hay. If you like old dark house movies and trains, then this is definitely for you.

strangely enough it's the kind of film that you'll want to see again and a

. . . .

```
eli5.show_prediction(model, corpus_train[4], vec=vectorizer,
                target_names=['Negative','Positive'])
# explain local prediction
```

y=Negative (probability **0.682**, score **-0.761**) top features

Contribution?	Feature
+0.935	Highlighted in text (sum)
-0.174	<BIAS>

how could 4 out of 16 prior voters give this movie a 10? How could more than half the prior voters give it a 7 or higher? Who is voting here? I can only assume it is primarily kids -- very young kids. the fact is that this is a bad movie in every way. the story is stupid; the acting is hard to even think of . . . .

```
eli5.show_prediction(model, corpus_train[100], vec=vectorizer,
                target_names=''Nagativ''''Positiv'']) #
explain local prediction
```

y=Negative (probability **0.757**, score **-1.139**) top features

Contribution?	Feature
+1.313	Highlighted in text (sum)
-0.174	<BIAS>

this movie was so poorly written and directed i fell asleep 30 minutes through the movie....................

The green patches show positive features for the target class `positive`, and the red parts are negative features that correspond to the `negative` class. The feature value and the weight value indicate the relative importance of words as features in classifying sentiments. It is observed that many stop words or unwanted words are present in the tokenization process; hence, they are appearing as features in the feature importance. The way to clean it up is to use preprocessing steps such as applying stemming, removing stop words, performing lemmatization, removing numbers, etc. Once the text cleanup is completed, then the previous recipes can be used again to create a better model to predict the sentiments.

Conclusion

In this chapter, we covered how to interpret the text classification use cases such as sentiment analysis. However, for all such kinds of use cases, the process will remain same, and the same recipes can be used. The modeling technique selection may change as the features increase, and we can use complex models such as ensemble modeling techniques like random forest, gradient boosting techniques, and catboost techniques. Also, the preprocessing methods can change. For example, the count vectorizer, TF-IDF vectorizer, hashing vectorizer, etc., can be applied with stop word removal to clean the text to get better features. The recipes to run different variants of ensemble models were covered in the previous chapter. In the next chapter, we are going to cover times-series model explainability.

CHAPTER 6

Explainability for Time-Series Models

A time series, as the name implies, has a time stamp and a variable that we are observing over time, such as stock prices, sales, revenue, profit over time, etc. Time-series modeling is a set of techniques that can be used to generate multistep predictions for a future time period, which will help a business to plan better and will help decision-makers to plan according to the future estimations. There are machine learning–based techniques that can be applied to generate future forecasting; also, there is a need to explain the predictions about the future.

The most commonly used techniques for time-series forecasting are autoregressive methods, moving average methods, autoregressive and moving average methods, and deep learning–based techniques such as LSTM, etc. The time-series model requires the data to be at frequent time intervals. If there is any gap in recording, it requires a different process to address the gap in the time series. The time-series model can be looked at from two ways: univariate, which is completely dependent on time, and multivariate, which takes into account various factors. Those factors are called *causal factors*, which impact the predictions. In the time-series model, the time is an independent variable, so

© Pradeepta Mishra 2023
P. Mishra, *Explainable AI Recipes*, https://doi.org/10.1007/978-1-4842-9029-3_6

we can compute various features from the time as an independent feature. Time-series modeling has various components such as trend, seasonality, and cyclicity.

Recipe 6-1. Explain Time-Series Models Using LIME

Problem

You want to explain a time-series model using LIME.

Solution

We are taking into consideration a sample dataset that has dates and prices, and we are going to consider only the univariate analysis. We will be using the LIME library to explain the predictions.

How It Works

Let's take a look at the following example (see Figure 6-1):

```
import pandas as pd
import numpy as np
import matplotlib.pyplot as plt
%matplotlib inline
df = pd.read_csv('https://raw.githubusercontent.com/
pradmishra1/PublicDatasets/main/monthly_csv.csv',index_col=0)

# seasonal difference
differenced = df.diff(12)
# trim off the first year of empty data
differenced = differenced[12:]
```

```
# save differenced dataset to file
differenced.to_csv('seasonally_adjusted.csv', index=False)
# plot differenced dataset
differenced.plot()
plt.show()
```

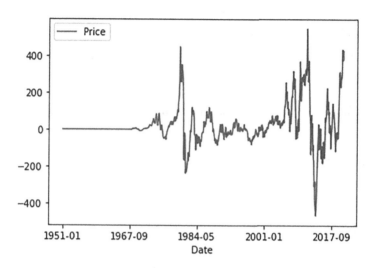

Figure 6-1. *Seasonally adjusted difference plot*

```
# reframe as supervised learning
dataframe = pd.DataFrame()
for i in range(12,0,-1):
    dataframe['t-'+str(i)] = df.shift(i).values[:,0]
dataframe['t'] = df.values[:,0]
print(dataframe.head(13))
dataframe = dataframe[13:]
# save to new file
dataframe.to_csv('lags_12months_features.csv', index=False)
```

For the last 12 months, lagged features will be used as training features to forecast the future time-series sales values.

```
# split into input and output
df = pd.read_csv('lags_12months_features.csv')
data = df.values
X = data[:,0:-1]
y = data[:,-1]

from sklearn.ensemble import RandomForestRegressor
# fit random forest model
model = RandomForestRegressor(n_estimators=500, random_state=1)
model.fit(X, y)
```

We are using a random forest regressor to consider the importance of each feature in a subset scenario. See Figure 6-2.

```
# show importance scores
print(model.feature_importances_)
# plot importance scores
names = dataframe.columns.values[0:-1]
ticks = [i for i in range(len(names))]
plt.bar(ticks, model.feature_importances_)
plt.xticks(ticks, names)
plt.show()
```

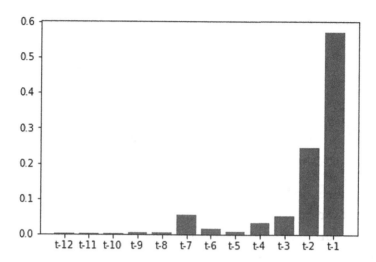

Figure 6-2. *Feature importance for lagged features from the 12 lagged features*

```
from sklearn.feature_selection import RFE
```

Recursive feature elimination is a technique usually used to fine-tune relevant features from the available list of features so that only important features can go into the inference generation process.

```
# perform feature selection
rfe = RFE(RandomForestRegressor(n_estimators=500, random_
state=1), n_features_to_select=4)
fit = rfe.fit(X, y)

# report selected features
print('Selected Features:')
names = dataframe.columns.values[0:-1]
for i in range(len(fit.support_)):
    if fit.support_[i]:
        print(names[i])
```

Selected Features:
t-7
t-3
t-2
t-1

We can rank the time-aware important features, which are lags. See Figure 6-3 and Figure 6-4.

```
# plot feature rank
names = dataframe.columns.values[0:-1]
ticks = [i for i in range(len(names))]
plt.bar(ticks, fit.ranking_)
plt.xticks(ticks, names)
plt.show()
```

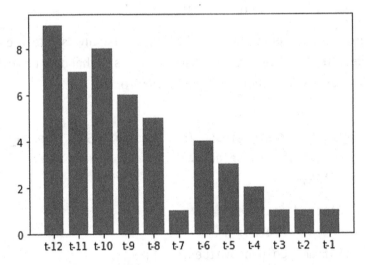

Figure 6-3. *Feature ranking from all available lags*

```
!pip install Lime

import lime
import lime.lime_tabular
explainer = lime.lime_tabular.LimeTabularExplainer(np.array(X),
                                    mode='regression',
                                    feature_names=X.columns,
                                    class_names=['t'],
                                    verbose=True)

explainer.feature_frequencies
{0: array([0.25659472, 0.24340528, 0.24940048, 0.25059952]),
 1: array([0.25539568, 0.24460432, 0.24940048, 0.25059952]),
 2: array([0.25419664, 0.24580336, 0.24940048, 0.25059952]),
 3: array([0.2529976 , 0.2470024 , 0.24940048, 0.25059952]), 4:
 array([0.25179856, 0.24820144, 0.24940048, 0.25059952]), 5:
 array([0.25059952, 0.24940048, 0.24940048, 0.25059952]), 6:
 array([0.2529976 , 0.2470024 , 0.24940048, 0.25059952]), 7:
 array([0.25179856, 0.24820144, 0.24940048, 0.25059952]), 8:
 array([0.25059952, 0.24940048, 0.24940048, 0.25059952]), 9:
 array([0.25059952, 0.24940048, 0.24940048, 0.25059952]), 10:
 array([0.25059952, 0.24940048, 0.24940048, 0.25059952]), 11:
 array([0.25059952, 0.24940048, 0.24940048, 0.25059952])}

# asking for explanation for LIME model
i = 60
exp = explainer.explain_instance(np.array(X)[i],
                                    new_model.predict,
                                    num_features=12
                                    )
```

```
Intercept 524.1907857658252
Prediction_local [76.53408383]
Right: 35.77034850521053
X does not have valid feature names, but LinearRegression was
fitted with feature names
```

```
exp.show_in_notebook(show_table=True)
```

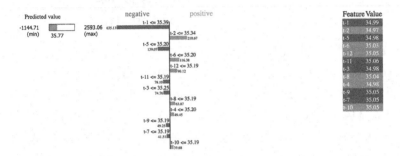

Figure 6-4. *Local interpretation for time series*

For the 60th record from the dataset, the predicted value is 35.77, for which lag 1 is the most important feature.

```
exp.as_list()
[('t-1 <= 35.39', -635.1332339969734), ('t-2 <= 35.34',
210.66614528187935), ('t-5 <= 35.20', -139.067880800616),
('t-6 <= 35.20', 116.37720395001742), ('t-12 <= 35.19',
90.11939668085971), ('t-11 <= 35.19', -78.09554990821964),
('t-3 <= 35.25', -74.75587075373902), ('t-8 <= 35.19',
63.86565747018194), ('t-4 <= 35.20', 49.45398090327778),
('t-9 <= 35.19', -49.24830755303888), ('t-7 <= 35.19',
-41.51328966914635), ('t-10 <= 35.19', 39.67504645890767)]
```

```
# Code for SP-LIME
import warnings
from lime import submodular_pick
```

```
# Remember to convert the dataframe to matrix values
# SP-LIME returns exaplanations on a sample set to provide a
non redundant global decision boundary of original model
sp_obj = submodular_pick.SubmodularPick(explainer, np.array(X),
                                new_model.predict,
                                num_features=12,
                                num_exps_desired=10)
```

The SP-LIME module from the LIME library provides explanations on a sample set to provide a global decision boundary about the prediction. In the previous script, we are considering the time-series model as a supervised learning model and using 12 lags as features. From the LIME library, we are using the LIME tabular explainer. The following script shows the explanation of record number 60. The predicted value is 35.77, and the lower threshold value and upper threshold value reflect the confidence band of the predicted outcome. Figure 6-5 shows the positive factors and negative factors contributing toward the prediction.

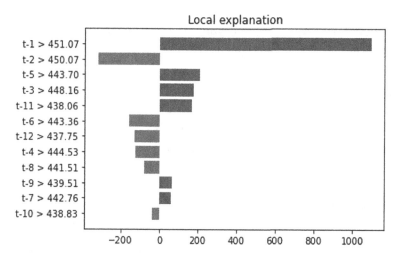

Figure 6-5. *The local explanation shows positive features in green and negative in red*

Recipe 6-2. Explain Time-Series Models Using SHAP

Problem

You want to explain the time-series model using SHAP.

Solution

We are taking into consideration a sample dataset that has dates and prices, and we are going to consider only the univariate analysis. We will be using the SHAP library to explain the predictions.

How It Works

Let's take a look at the following example (Figure 6-6):

```
import shap
from sklearn.ensemble import RandomForestRegressor
rforest = RandomForestRegressor(n_estimators=100, random_
state=0)
rforest.fit(X, y)

# explain all the predictions in the test set
explainer = shap.TreeExplainer(rforest)
shap_values = explainer.shap_values(X)

shap.summary_plot(shap_values, X)
```

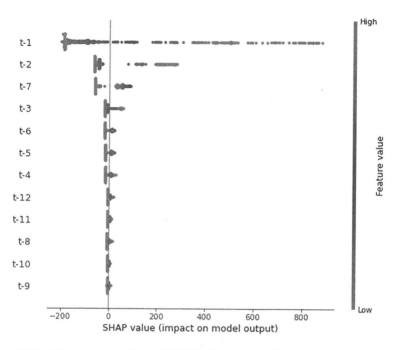

Figure 6-6. *Summary plot of SHAP feature values*

t-1, t-2, and t-7 are the three important features that impact the predictions. t-1 means a lag of the last time period, t-2 means a lag of the past two time periods, and t-7 means a lag of the seventh time period. Let's say data is available at a monthly level, so t-1 means last month, t-2 means the second month in the past, and t-7 means the seventh month in the past. These values impact the predictions. See Figure 6-7 and Figure 6-8.

```
shap.dependence_plot("t-1", shap_values, X)
```

229

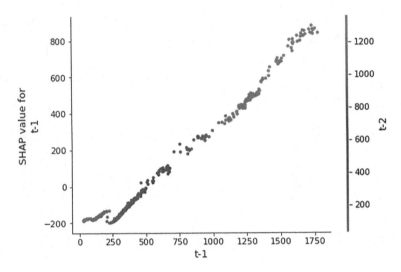

Figure 6-7. *SHAP dependence plot*

```
shap.partial_dependence_plot(
  "t-1", rforest.predict, X, ice=False,
  model_expected_value=True, feature_expected_value=True
)
```

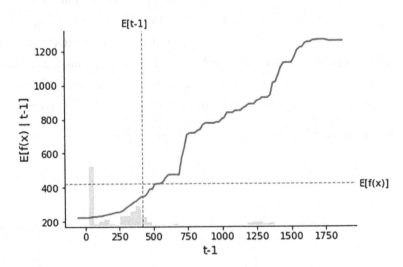

Figure 6-8. *Partial dependence plot for feature t-1*

Conclusion

In this chapter, we covered how to interpret a time-series model to generate a forecast. To interpret a univariate time-series model, we considered it as a supervised learning problem by taking the lags as trainable features. These features are then trained using a linear regressor, and the regression model is used to generate explanations at a global level as well as at a local level using both the SHAP and LIME libraries. A similar explanation can be generated using more complex algorithms such as the nonlinear and ensemble techniques, and finally similar kinds of graphs and charts can be generated using SHAP and LIME as in the previous chapters. The next chapter contains recipes to explain deep neural network models.

CHAPTER 7

Explainability for Deep Learning Models

Deep learning models are becoming the backbone of artificial intelligence implementations. At the same time, it is super important to build the explainability layers to explain the predictions and output of the deep learning model. To build trust for the deep learning model outcome, we need to explain the results or output. At a high level, a deep learning layer involves more than one hidden layer, whereas a neural network layer has three layers: the input layer, the hidden layer, and the output layer. There are different variants of neural network models such as single hidden layer neural network model, multiple hidden layer neural networks, feedforward neural networks, and backpropagation neural networks. Depending upon the structure of the neural network model, there are three popular structures: recurrent neural networks, which are mostly used for sequential information processing, such as audio processing, text classification, etc.; deep neural networks, which are used for building extremely deep networks; and finally, convolutional neural network models, which are used for image classification.

Deep SHAP is a framework to derive the SHAP values from a deep learning model developed using TensorFlow, Keras, or PyTorch. If we compare the machine learning models with deep learning models,

© Pradeepta Mishra 2023
P. Mishra, *Explainable AI Recipes*, https://doi.org/10.1007/978-1-4842-9029-3_7

the deep learning models are too difficult to explain to anyone. In this chapter, we will provide recipes for explaining the components of a deep learning model.

Recipe 7-1. Explain MNIST Images Using a Gradient Explainer Based on Keras

Problem

You want to explain a Keras-based deep learning model using SHAP.

Solution

We are using a sample image dataset called MNIST. We can first train a convolutional neural network using Keras from the TensorFlow pipeline. Then we can use the gradient explainer module from the SHAP library to build the explainer object. The explainer object can be used to create SHAP values, and further, using SHAP values, we can get more visibility into image classification tasks and individual class prediction and corresponding probability values.

How It Works

Let's take a look at the following example:

```
import TensorFlow as tf
from TensorFlow.keras import Input
from TensorFlow.keras.layers import Flatten, Dense,
Dropout, Conv2D
import warnings
warnings.filterwarnings("ignore")
```

```
# load the MNIST data
(x_train, y_train), (x_test, y_test) = tf.keras.datasets.mnist.
load_data()
x_train, x_test = x_train / 255.0, x_test / 255.0
x_train = x_train.astype('float32')
x_test = x_test.astype('float32')
x_train = x_train.reshape(x_train.shape[0], 28, 28, 1)
x_test = x_test.reshape(x_test.shape[0], 28, 28, 1)
```

There are two inputs: one for generating explanations using a feedforward neural network layer and another using the convolutional neural network layer. This is to compare the two inputs that can be explained by the SHAP library in different ways.

```
# define our model
input1 = Input(shape=(28,28,1))
input2 = Input(shape=(28,28,1))
input2c = Conv2D(32, kernel_size=(3, 3), activation='relu')
(input2)
joint = tf.keras.layers.concatenate([Flatten()(input1),
Flatten()(input2c)])
out = Dense(10, activation='softmax')(Dropout(0.2)(Dense(128,
activation='relu')(joint)))
model = tf.keras.models.Model(inputs = [input1, input2],
outputs=out)
model.summary()
```

```
Model: "model"
```

Layer (type)	Output Shape	Param #	Connected to
input_2 (InputLayer)	[(None, 28, 28, 1)]	0	[]
input_1 (InputLayer)	[(None, 28, 28, 1)]	0	[]
conv2d (Conv2D)	(None, 26, 26, 32)	320	['input_2[0][0]']
flatten (Flatten)	(None, 784)	0	['input_1[0][0]']
flatten_1 (Flatten)	(None, 21632)	0	['conv2d[0][0]']
concatenate (Concatenate)	(None, 22416)	0	['flatten[0][0]', 'flatten_1[0][0]']
dense_1 (Dense)	(None, 128)	2869376	['concatenate[0][0]']
dropout (Dropout)	(None, 128)	0	['dense_1[0][0]']
dense (Dense)	(None, 10)	1290	['dropout[0][0]']

```
Total params: 2,870,986
Trainable params: 2,870,986
Non-trainable params: 0
```

Compile the model using the Adam optimizer, with sparse categorical cross entropy and accuracy. We can choose different types of optimizers to achieve the best accuracy.

```
model.compile(optimizer='adam',
            loss='sparse_categorical_crossentropy',
            metrics=['accuracy'])
```

As the next step, we can train the model. An epoch of 3 has been selected due to processing constraints, but the epoch size can be increased based on the time availability and the computational power of the machines.

```
# fit the model
model.fit([x_train, x_train], y_train, epochs=3)
```

Once the model is created, in the next step we can install the SHAP library and create a gradient explainer object either using the same training dataset or using the test dataset.

236

```
pip install shap
import shap

# since we have two inputs we pass a list of inputs to the
explainer
explainer = shap.GradientExplainer(model, [x_train, x_train])

# we explain the model's predictions on the first three samples
of the test set
shap_values = explainer.shap_values([x_test[:3], x_test[:3]])

# since the model has 10 outputs we get a list of 10
explanations (one for each output)
print(len(shap_values))
```

The two inputs were explained previously. There are two set of SHAP values, one corresponding to the feedforward layer and another relating to the convolutional neural network layer. See Figure 7-1 and Figure 7-2.

```
# since the model has 2 inputs we get a list of 2 explanations
(one for each input) for each output
print(len(shap_values[0]))

# here we plot the explanations for all classes for the first
input (this is the feed forward input)
shap.image_plot([shap_values[i][0] for i in range(10)],
x_test[:3])
```

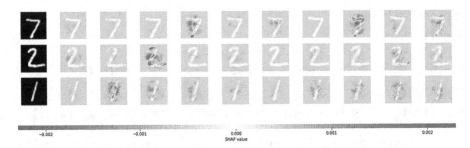

Figure 7-1. *SHAP value for three samples with positive and negative weights*

```
# here we plot the explanations for all classes for the second
input (this is the conv-net input)
shap.image_plot([shap_values[i][1] for i in range(10)],
x_test[:3])
```

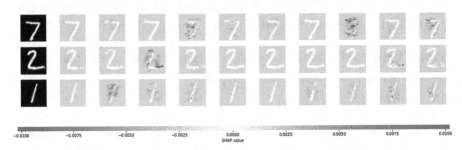

Figure 7-2. *SHAP value for the second input versus all classes*

```
# get the variance of our estimates
shap_values, shap_values_var = explainer.shap_values
([x_test[:3], x_test[:3]], return_variances=True)
```

To explain the feedforward way of weight distribution and attribution of classes, we need to estimate the variances; hence, we need to get the SHAP values of variances. See Figure 7-3.

```
# here we plot the explanations for all classes for the first
input (this is the feed forward input)
shap.image_plot([shap_values_var[i][0] for i in range(10)],
x_test[:3])
```

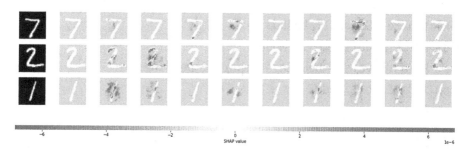

Figure 7-3. *Feedforward input explanations for all classes*

Recipe 7-2. Use Kernel Explainer–Based SHAP Values from a Keras Model

Problem

You want to explain the kernel-based explainer for a structured data problem for binary classification, while training with a deep learning model from Keras.

Solution

We will use the census income dataset, which is available in the SHAP library; develop a neural network model; and then use the trained model object to apply the kernel explainer. The kernel SHAP method is defined as a special weighted linear regression to compute the importance of each feature in a deep learning model.

How It Works

Let's take a look at the following example:

```
from sklearn.model_selection import train_test_split
from keras.layers import Input, Dense, Flatten, Concatenate,
concatenate, Dropout, Lambda
from keras.models import Model
from keras.layers.embeddings import Embedding
from tqdm import tqdm
import shap

# print the JS visualization code to the notebook
#shap.initjs()
```

If the machine supports JS visualization, then please remove the comment and run the previous script. See Figure 7-4.

```
X,y = shap.datasets.adult()
X_display,y_display = shap.datasets.adult(display=True)

# normalize data (this is important for model convergence)
dtypes = list(zip(X.dtypes.index, map(str, X.dtypes)))
for k,dtype in dtypes:
    if dtype == "float32":
        X[k] -= X[k].mean()
        X[k] /= X[k].std()

X_train, X_valid, y_train, y_valid = train_test_split(X, y,
test_size=0.2, random_state=7)

# build model
input_els = []
encoded_els = []
for k,dtype in dtypes:
```

```
    input_els.append(Input(shape=(1,)))
    if dtype == "int8":
        e = Flatten()(Embedding(X_train[k].max()+1, 1)
        (input_els[-1]))
    else:
        e = input_els[-1]
    encoded_els.append(e)
encoded_els = concatenate(encoded_els)
layer1 = Dropout(0.5)(Dense(100, activation="relu")
(encoded_els))
out = Dense(1)(layer1)

# train model
clf = Model(inputs=input_els, outputs=[out])
clf.compile(optimizer="adam", loss='binary_crossentropy')
clf.fit(
    [X_train[k].values for k,t in dtypes],
    y_train,
    epochs=5,
    batch_size=512,
    shuffle=True,
    validation_data=([X_valid[k].values for k,t in dtypes],
    y_valid)
)

def f(X):
    return clf.predict([X[:,i] for i in range(X.shape[1])]).
    flatten()

# print the JS visualization code to the notebook
shap.initjs()

explainer = shap.KernelExplainer(f, X.iloc[:50,:])
```

```
shap_values = explainer.shap_values(X.iloc[299,:],
nsamples=500)
```

To generate the SHAP values, we need to use the kernel explainer function from the SHAP library.

```
shap_values50 = explainer.shap_values(X.iloc[280:285,:],
nsamples=500)
shap_values
```

```
import warnings
warnings.filterwarnings("ignore")
# summarize the effects of all the features
shap_values50 = explainer.shap_values(X.iloc[280:781,:],
nsamples=500)
```

```
shap.summary_plot(shap_values50)
```

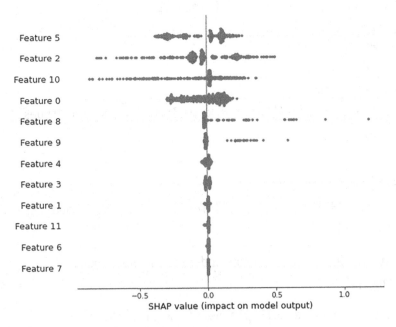

Figure 7-4. *SHAP values feature importance*

Recipe 7-3. Explain a PyTorch-Based Deep Learning Model

Problem

You want to explain a deep learning model developed using PyTorch.

Solution

We are using a tool called Captum, which acts as a platform. Different kinds of explainability methods are embedded into Captum that help to further elaborate on how a decision has been made. A typical neural network model interpretation can be done to understand the feature importance, dominant layer identification, and dominant neuron identification. Captum provides three attribution algorithms that help in achieving three things: primary attribution, layer attribution, and neuron attribution.

How It Works

The following syntax explains how to install the library:

```
conda install captum -c pytorch
```

or

```
pip install captum
```

The primary attribution layer provides integrated gradients, gradient shapely additive explanations (SHAP), saliency, etc., to interpret the model in a more effective way. We can use sample data as titanic survival prediction dataset, which is a common dataset that is used for machine learning examples or tutorials every developer can quickly relate to it without much introduction.

```python
# Initial imports
import numpy as np

import torch

from captum.attr import IntegratedGradients
from captum.attr import LayerConductance
from captum.attr import NeuronConductance

import matplotlib
import matplotlib.pyplot as plt
%matplotlib inline

from scipy import stats
import pandas as pd
dataset_path = "https://raw.githubusercontent.com/pradmishra1/
PublicDatasets/main/titanic.csv"

titanic_data = pd.read_csv(dataset_path)
del titanic_data['Unnamed: 0']
del titanic_data['PassengerId']
titanic_data = pd.concat([titanic_data,
                          pd.get_dummies(titanic_data['Sex']),
                          pd.get_dummies(titanic_data['Embarked
                          '],prefix="embark"),
                          pd.get_dummies(titanic_data['Pclass'],
                          prefix="class")], axis=1)
titanic_data["Age"] = titanic_data["Age"].fillna(titanic_
data["Age"].mean())
titanic_data["Fare"] = titanic_data["Fare"].fillna(titanic_
data["Fare"].mean())
titanic_data = titanic_data.drop(['Name','Ticket','Cabin','Sex',
'Embarked','Pclass'], axis=1)
```

```
# Set random seed for reproducibility.
np.random.seed(707)

# Convert features and labels to numpy arrays.
labels = titanic_data["Survived"].to_numpy()
titanic_data = titanic_data.drop(['Survived'], axis=1)
feature_names = list(titanic_data.columns)
data = titanic_data.to_numpy()

# Separate training and test sets using
train_indices = np.random.choice(len(labels),
int(0.7*len(labels)), replace=False)
test_indices = list(set(range(len(labels))) - set(train_
indices))
train_features = data[train_indices]
train_labels = labels[train_indices]
test_features = data[test_indices]
test_labels = labels[test_indices]
train_features.shape
(623, 12)
```

Now that the train and test datasets are ready, we can start writing the code for the model development using PyTorch.

```
Import torch
import torch.nn as nn
torch.manual_seed(1)  # Set seed for reproducibility.
Class TitanicSimpleNNModel(nn.Module):
    def __init__(self):
        super().__init__()
        self.linear1 = nn.Linear(12, 12)
        self.sigmoid1 = nn.Sigmoid()
        self.linear2 = nn.Linear(12, 8)
```

```
        self.sigmoid2 = nn.Sigmoid()
        self.linear3 = nn.Linear(8, 2)
        self.softmax = nn.Softmax(dim=1)

    def forward(self, x):
        lin1_out = self.linear1(x)
        sigmoid_out1 = self.sigmoid1(lin1_out)
        sigmoid_out2 = self.sigmoid2(self.
        linear2(sigmoid_out1))
        return self.softmax(self.linear3(sigmoid_out2))

net = TitanicSimpleNNModel()
criterion = nn.CrossEntropyLoss()
num_epochs = 200

optimizer = torch.optim.Adam(net.parameters(), lr=0.1)
input_tensor = torch.from_numpy(train_features).type(torch.
FloatTensor)
label_tensor = torch.from_numpy(train_labels)
```

The deep learning model configuration is done, so we can proceed with running epochs or iterations to reduce the errors.

```
For epoch in range(num_epochs):
  output = net(input_tensor)
  loss = criterion(output, label_tensor)
  optimizer.zero_grad()
  loss.backward()
  optimizer.step()
  if epoch % 20 == 0:
        print ('Epoch {}/{} => Loss: {:.2f}'.format(epoch+1,
        num_epochs, loss.item()))
torch.save(net.state_dict(), '/model.pt')
```

```
Epoch 1/200 => Loss: 0.70
Epoch 21/200 => Loss: 0.55
Epoch 41/200 => Loss: 0.50
Epoch 61/200 => Loss: 0.49
Epoch 81/200 => Loss: 0.48
Epoch 101/200 => Loss: 0.49
Epoch 121/200 => Loss: 0.47
Epoch 141/200 => Loss: 0.47
Epoch 161/200 => Loss: 0.47
Epoch 181/200 => Loss: 0.47
```

```
out_probs = net(input_tensor).detach().numpy()
out_classes = np.argmax(out_probs, axis=1)
print("Train Accuracy:", sum(out_classes == train_labels) /
len(train_labels))
Train Accuracy: 0.8523274478330658
```

```
test_input_tensor = torch.from_numpy(test_features).type(torch.
FloatTensor)
out_probs = net(test_input_tensor).detach().numpy()
out_classes = np.argmax(out_probs, axis=1)
print("Test Accuracy:", sum(out_classes == test_labels) /
len(test_labels))
```

```
Test Accuracy: 0.832089552238806
```

The integrated gradient is extracted from the neural network model; this can be done using the `attribute` function.

```
ig = IntegratedGradients(net)
test_input_tensor.requires_grad_()
attr, delta = ig.attribute(test_input_tensor,target=1,
return_convergence_delta=True)
attr = attr.detach().numpy()
```

```
np.round(attr,2)
array([[-0.7 , 0.09, -0. , ..., 0. , 0. , -0.33], [-2.78, -0. ,
-0. , ..., 0. , 0. , -1.82], [-0.65, 0. , -0. , ..., 0. , 0. ,
-0.31], ..., [-0.47, -0. , -0. , ..., 0.71, 0. , -0. ], [-0.1 ,
-0. , -0. , ..., 0. , 0. , -0.1 ], [-0.7 , 0. , -0. , ..., 0. ,
0. , -0.28]])
```

The attr object contains the feature importance of the input features from the model.

```
importances = np.mean(attr, axis=0)
for i in range(len(feature_names)):
        print(feature_names[i], ": ", '%.3f'%(importances[i]))
Age :   -0.574
SibSp :   -0.010
Parch :   -0.026
Fare :   0.278
female :   0.101
male :   -0.460
embark_C :   0.042
embark_Q :   0.005
embark_S :   -0.021
class_1 :   0.067
class_2 :   0.090
class_3 :   -0.144
```

The LayerConductance helps us compute the neuron importance and combines the neuron activation by taking the partial derivative of the neuron with respect to the input and output. The conductance layer builds on the integrated gradients by looking at the flow of IG attribution.

```
cond = LayerConductance(net, net.sigmoid1)
```

```
cond_vals = cond.attribute(test_input_tensor,target=1)
cond_vals = cond_vals.detach().numpy()
Average_Neuron_Importances = np.mean(cond_vals, axis=0)
Average_Neuron_Importances
array([ 0.03051018, -0.23244175, 0.04743345, 0.02102091,
-0.08071412, -0.09040915, -0.13398956, -0.04666219, 0.03577907,
-0.07206058, -0.15658873, 0.03491106], dtype=float32)

neuron_cond = NeuronConductance(net, net.sigmoid1)

neuron_cond_vals_10 = neuron_cond.attribute(test_input_tensor,
neuron_selector=10, target=1)
neuron_cond_vals_0 = neuron_cond.attribute(test_input_tensor,
neuron_selector=0, target=1)
# Average Feature Importances for Neuron 0
nn0 = neuron_cond_vals_0.mean(dim=0).detach().numpy()
np.round(nn0,3)
array([ 0.008, 0. , 0. , 0.028, 0. , -0.004, -0. , 0. , -0.001,
-0. , 0. , -0. ], dtype=float32)
```

The average feature importance for neuron 0 can be replicated to any number of neurons by using a threshold. If the weight threshold exceeds a certain level, then the neuron attribution and average feature importance for that neuron can be derived.

Conclusion

In this chapter, we looked two frameworks, SHAP and Captum, to explain a deep learning model developed either using Keras or using PyTorch. The more we parse the information using these libraries and take a smaller chunk of data, the more visibility we will get into how the model works, how the model makes prediction, and how the model makes an attribution to a local instance.

To review, this book started with explaining linear supervised models for both regression and classification tasks, then explained nonlinear decision tree–based models, and then covered the ensemble models such as bagging, boosting, and stacking. Finally, we ended the book with explaining the times-series model, natural language processing–based text classification, and deep neural network–based models.

Index

Printed in the United States
by Baker & Taylor Publisher Services